GARY LIBRARY

VERMONT

✓ P9-DYY-516

WITHDRAWN

WITHDRAWN

THE AMERICAN HIGH SCHOOL
TODAY

THE AMERICAN HIGH SCHOOL TODAY

A First Report to Interested Citizens
by **JAMES BRYANT CONANT**

WITHDRAWN

McGRAW-HILL BOOK COMPANY, INC.
New York   Toronto   London

THE AMERICAN HIGH SCHOOL TODAY

Copyright © 1959 by James Bryant Conant.
Printed in the United States of America.
All rights reserved. This book or parts
thereof may not be reproduced in any form
without written permission of the publishers.

Library of Congress Catalog Card Number: 59–8527

First Edition

Second Printing, February 1959

This volume is the first in a projected series of publications
to be known as the Carnegie Series in American Education.
Subsequent titles and authors will be announced at a later
date.

373.7
C743a
c.5

ACKNOWLEDGMENT

Pub. McGaw 1959 2.55 V.C. Alumni

I was fortunate, in organizing this study of the American high school, in being able to enlist the services of four able co-workers, two of whom had had years of experience in high school administration. In my visits to schools, I always had the valuable assistance of at least one co-worker. Although the opinions expressed in this report are my own, I believe that, in general, they also reflect the views of my four colleagues; certainly, their accumulated wisdom and effective labors have shaped to no small degree the findings of this report and my recommendations. With pleasant memories of many hours of stimulating discussions and long journeys, I record my indebtedness to my four collaborators: Eugene Youngert, Bernard S. Miller, Nathaniel Ober, Reuben H. Gross.

When I first planned the study, I had in mind formulating my conclusions in such a way that they could be presented in various states to the citizens committees concerned with supporting good public education. I discussed these plans with the officers of the National Citizens Council for Better Schools, who promised to assist me in meeting with citizens groups in different sections of the country. During the past months a number of such meetings have taken place, and I should like to thank Henry Toy, Jr., President of the National Citizens Council for Better Schools, and his associates for their cooperation in making the arrangements.

The study has been made possible by a generous grant from the Carnegie Corporation of New York to the Edu-

10220

cational Testing Service of Princeton, New Jersey, on my behalf. I wish to record my appreciation of the Corporation's support and for the help of Henry Chauncey, John S. Hollister, and the other officers and staff members of the Educational Testing Service in providing the logistic support of this enterprise. I am indebted to E. Alden Dunham for assistance in preparing the manuscript for publication. In particular, I wish to thank Betty Jane Watkins for her invaluable help as manager of our office in New York.

James B. Conant

A Study of the American High School
588 Fifth Avenue
New York 36, N. Y.

November 10, 1958

CONTENTS

APPENDIXES

FOREWORD

On February 19, 1957, James Bryant Conant performed his final duties as United States Ambassador to the Federal Republic of Germany. Ten days later he was absorbed in the initial stages of this history-making study of the American high school.

The preparations for the change had already been laid. Many months before, I had asked Mr. Conant whether there was any possibility that he might turn his attention to education after completing his tour of duty in Germany. He responded that a return to the field of education was uppermost in his mind and that the thing he wished most to do was to examine some of the critical problems facing the American high school.

His answer was good news for American education. It would be hard to find anyone better equipped to make such a study at this moment in our history. At the summit of a career of distinguished service to education and to the nation, Mr. Conant's capacity to command public confidence is great and well deserved. His devotion to rigorous intellectual training and his dedication to the social and political principles which animate this nation are both vitally important qualifications for the job.

The focus of Mr. Conant's study is the "comprehensive" high school—a peculiarly American phenomenon. It is called comprehensive because it offers, under one administration and under one roof (or series of roofs), secondary education for almost all the high school age children of one town or neighborhood. It is responsible for educating the boy who will be an atomic scientist and the girl who will marry at eighteen; the prospective captain of a ship and the future captain of industry. It is responsible for educating the bright and the not so bright children with different vocational and professional ambitions and with various motivations. It is responsible, in sum, for providing good and appropriate education, both academic and vocational, for all young people within a democratic environment which the American people believe serves the principles they cherish.

There are those who say it cannot be done. When a man like James Conant says it *can* be done, the nation must take notice.

When Mr. Conant was still a very young man, he was recognized as one of the nation's great chemists. He was president of Harvard University at forty. He served not only Harvard but the nation in both world wars. He has been a lifelong student not only of American education but also of comparative education, and has made intensive studies of Australian, New Zealand, British, German, and Swiss schools. Mr. Conant's appointment to one of our highest diplomatic posts in 1953 might have been thought by some to be the closing chapter in a brilliant career. But the chapter which followed was to give a new and exciting turn to the story.

When Mr. Conant departed from high public office, he also chose deliberately to step out of the limelight. He turned down innumerable speaking invitations. He refused many requests from distinguished organizations to serve on boards of trustees and directors. As much as possible, he avoided all of the varied honors and tributes that come to a man in his position. He was too busy.

He drew up his plans with a swift, sure hand. He assembled a topnotch staff. And he was soon in the field gathering information. All of this was before the appearance of the Russian satellites led the American people to take a fresh look at their educational system. Like all people who had given serious and sustained attention to American education, Mr. Conant had nothing to learn about this subject from the Russian satellites. He was already a highly informed and discriminating friend of the best in American education. He undertook the study precisely because of his comprehension of the problems facing the American high school and his profound conviction that these problems could be dealt with.

Unlike some observers, Mr. Conant makes little use of comparisons with Russian education. The surge of publicity about Soviet schools has produced more false impressions and foolish conclusions than almost any other element in current discussions of education. Sensible generalizations about Russian schools are made doubly difficult by the recent switches in Soviet educational policy. The future direction of Russian education is not clear. And even if we knew exactly where Soviet education was going, the information would be of limited relevance. It is impossible to evaluate an educational system apart from the society which it both reflects and serves. Mr. Conant understands this, and he has repeatedly emphasized that American education must keep its eye on its own goals and be strong in its own terms.

This is a down-to-earth report. It deals with matters of fact and its recommendations are specific. It will be of interest chiefly to those who are realistic enough to face the problems of education in American society as these problems now exist. Much of the argument over education today is coming from people who are *not* really interested in facing problems as they exist. They are interested in venting their prejudices or in beating one another about the ears with slogans and battle cries. If the reader belongs in this group, he will find little nourishment here. But if he is in the mood to roll up his sleeves and say "Precisely what can we do tomorrow morning to improve our schools?"—this is his book.

At points this report may appear educationally conservative in not commenting on promising experiments in areas such as educational television, or on new approaches to the teaching of mathematics, physics, and languages. But Mr. Conant's standing as a forward-looking educator needs no defense. Over the years he has shown a lively interest in school and college experimentation. This report makes only passing reference to the innovations mentioned simply because they will have to pass the test of time. In the present report Mr. Conant concentrates on those improvements in curriculum and school organization which can now be adopted with confidence by any school system.

In the last two years there has been a clamor of voices telling us what is wrong with our schools. The distinctive feature of Mr. Conant's contribution is that he has come forward with a positive and constructive approach. He emphasizes over and over that our average schools can become good schools, and our good schools excellent, by a series of steps easily grasped by any informed American.

It would be difficult to overestimate the importance of such a report at this time. Hundreds of thousands of Americans all over the country are concerned about their schools, wondering what to do about them, seeking answers, hoping for guidance. Mr. Conant has provided that guidance. It is for this reason that some of us believe that Mr. Conant, after a lifetime of distinguished contributions to the nation, has in this study made his greatest contribution of all.

There is no phase of our national life which could not be substantially improved through greater expenditure of effort on the part of the American people and through steadfast adherence to higher standards. This is true of our schools. They too can be improved. They too can rise to a

higher standard of excellence. It is Mr. Conant's intention
that they do so, and every serious friend of American education will applaud that intention.

If I had to recommend a single piece of reading to all
Americans who want to improve their schools, I would ask
them to read this report.

John W. Gardner, PRESIDENT
CARNEGIE CORPORATION OF NEW YORK

THE AMERICAN HIGH SCHOOL TODAY

SECTION I

The Characteristics
of American Education

The school board members and the school administrators to whom this report is directed are familiar with the basic assumptions underlying the present pattern of American education. They realize that the task of the American high school is a task which arises out of the historical developments of our schools, colleges, and universities and, in particular, reflects certain basic changes in the structure of our society which have occurred during this century. Some readers of this report, however, who have had little or no opportunity to study American public schools may not be aware of the processes by which our school and college arrangements have come to diverge so markedly from those in other free nations. Therefore, as an introduction to a study of one segment of the educational pattern—the tax-supported high school—a brief summary of the characteristics of American public education may be in order.

To a foreign observer several aspects of the American educational scene seem so strange as to be almost incomprehensible. First of all, our colleges and universities are baffling. There are so many institutions with so great a variety of requirements for admission and with so many different types of program that a foreign visitor has difficulty in identifying those portions of a university which are concerned with what he regards as the true university function. In European universities there is no equivalent of our undergraduate liberal arts college, no provision for general education. European universities are essentially a collection of faculties concerned with the education of future members of the learned professions. The general or liberal education of the doctor, lawyer, theologian, engineer, scientist, or professional scholar is provided by special secondary schools, admission to which is determined by a highly selective procedure at age ten or eleven. Not more than 20 per cent of an age group are selected from the elementary school and enrolled in the preuniversity schools. Therefore there is a waste of talent under the European system. No one has estimated how much potential talent goes undeveloped in Germany, France, Italy, and Switzerland because of the early selection of the preuniversity students—a selection often influenced by the class system of European lands. The other 80 to 85 per cent stop their formal education at age fourteen and go to work. Of course, the selection of those who are to be enrolled in the preuniversity school is on the basis of academic ability, but family tradition plays a big role and many boys and girls from the farm and working class never even think of trying to enter a preuniversity school.

In the European preuniversity schools an eight- or nine-year rigorous course in languages, mathematics, science, history, and literature prepares the student to pass a state examination for a certificate which admits him to a university. The failures during the long course are many, and a considerable number fall by the wayside, but those who succeed finish with a mastery of two foreign languages, a knowledge of mathematics through calculus and of physics and chemistry at the level of our sophomore college courses. Those who are not enrolled in the preuniversity schools, except for a small fraction who enter an intermediate school, complete their full-time education at age fourteen.

One often sees a comparison made between the proportion of the youth of college age who are studying in an American college or university and the proportion of German, or Swiss, or French youth who are attending a university. It is true that something like a third of our young people are "going to college," and only about a fifteenth or twentieth of the boys and girls in a European country are university students. But the vast majority of the Americans are *not* university students in the European sense of the term—that is, students preparing for a profession. Actually, the percentage of young men who are preparing to be doctors, lawyers, engineers, scientists, scholars, and teachers of academic subjects is about the same in this country as in Europe—a surprisingly small percentage, by the way —something like 6 per cent of an age group.

To understand American colleges and universities, one must be aware of their history. The existence of a few American four-year colleges during colonial days and the persistence of these institutions during the early years of the American republic have had a determining influence on higher education in this country. Of perhaps equal significance has been the movement to establish agricultural and mechanical arts colleges which started just about a century ago. The passage of the Morrill Act during the Civil War provided federal support for a new type of college in each state, the "land-grant colleges," as they were soon called. As these institutions developed, collegiate instruction in such practical fields as animal husbandry came to have the same academic standing as that of education for the professions. A proliferation of professional and semiprofessional areas of instruction, running from architecture to wild life conservation, started in the closing decades of the last cen-

tury and has continued in this century until today a cata-
logue of many an institution (privately controlled or pub-
licly supported) bears little resemblance to a corresponding
pamphlet issued by a European university.

The widening of the fields of instruction in the nineteenth century was part of a drastic educational reform that
was taking place on both sides of the Atlantic. The main
objective of this reform was the recognition of the physical
and biological sciences as reputable subjects to be studied
in a university. On this continent, because of the special
history of the American people, the movement took on
many special characteristics. The definition of what was a
"university subject" widened and widened as the decades
passed.

As the fields of study of applied science and practical
subjects broadened at the university level, instruction at the
secondary level also changed. A hundred years ago one
assumed a lawyer would have studied Greek and Latin; it
was argued that a classical education was essential for him
as a professional man. Fifty years later, it was hard to make
a convincing case that the preprofessional education of an
electrical engineer or an agriculturist should include instruction in reading Latin. And at no time in the educational history of this country has mastery of a modern foreign language come to be recognized as the hallmark of a
well-educated man or woman.

The transformation of the European university tradition on this continent is a theme about which much has
been written. But the impact of this mutation on the high
school seems at times to have been overlooked. Having
spent considerable time talking to university professors and
schoolteachers in several European countries, I have been
impressed by the basic differences in the total pattern of
tax-supported education on the two sides of the Atlantic.
And, having tried to explain American public education

to German audiences, I am aware of some of the peculiarities of our system—peculiar from a European standpoint. Yet I have found that by pointing out certain differences between American and European history one can lead a German, for example, to a better understanding of our schools (and also of some of our political institutions, but that is another story).

When Thomas Jefferson wrote of equality, he was certainly thinking of political equality. It is clear that the contrast between a new society without hereditary titles and an old society with an aristocracy was what he had in mind. The absence of conqueror and conquered, of a feudal system in our history, when pointed out to a European, provides a clue to understanding something of our present situation. So too does a realization of the importance of the pioneer movement westward in the nineteenth century. Frontiers—in the American sense of the term—have had no influence on the development of European nations, but the American frontier has in fact shaped our institutions. To a large extent, it was responsible for widening the concept of equality. For the American of the nineteenth century equality became, above all, equality of opportunity—an equal start in a competitive struggle. This aspect of equality acted like a magnet on inhabitants of other lands and attracted those immigrants whose settling on this continent so enriched our culture and invigorated our stock. And this wave of immigration placed on our tax-supported schools many educational tasks of a special nature. This fact is recognized by European educators who have studied our educational history, and more than one of them has spoken to me of the success of our public schools in bringing together the children of so many diverse peoples.

Equality thus came to mean for many new Americans not only political equality but also equality of opportunity. It came to mean too, especially west of the Alleghenies, equality of status of all honest labor. The land-grant colleges were both a symbol of equality of status and a means to the realization of the idea. One academic manifestation of this doctrine is our unwillingness to state frankly that a bachelor's degree has long since lost any meaning as a mark of scholastic attainment or the completion of a course of formal academic training. Whether one has a degree in engineering, agriculture, home economics, commerce, physical education, or in the arts and sciences, he is entitled to be called a "college graduate."

It is important to remember that the contrast between American and European education at the college and university level is nothing new. Except in terms of numbers, the differences were almost as great at the beginning of the century as they are now. Although only 4 per cent of the American youth were then attending a college or university compared to over 35 per cent today, the situation was as surprising to a European then as now. He then saw, as he still sees, a multitude of colleges and universities having no uniform standards for admission or for graduation, even in professional fields, and offering a wide range of practical subjects in which a student could major.

In the half-century that has elapsed, there have been no drastic changes in the basic pattern of education in either Europe or the United States. But in two respects the American pattern has diverged even more from that to be found in other countries; certain unique characteristics have been emphasized, so to speak. The percentage of youth attending a college or university has jumped from 4 to 35, and, at the same time, the percentage enrolled in grades eleven to twelve of the high school has about doubled. In 1910, only 35 per cent of the seventeen-year-olds were in school; today, the corresponding figure is over 70 per cent. These changes could easily have been predicted in 1900 by a student of American education. He would already have seen how enormous was the power of the twin ideals of equality of opportunity and equality of status; it was evident that the American people had come to believe that more education provided the means by which these ideals were to be realized. But two other factors also played a role. First, there was the urge for institutional expansion—the drive for larger faculties and student bodies in the colleges and universities; fifty years ago expansion was more than welcomed. Second, there was a radical change in the picture regarding the employment of youth. When this century began, approximately half of the boys and girls fifteen years of age were *not* attending school; many were at work. Thirty years later the percentage of this group attending school had reached 85. This alteration was not a consequence of state laws raising the school-leaving age; the laws were rather a consequence of profound economic and social changes. To explore adequately the background of this shift in the American scene would require many pages; suffice it to remind the reader that in the second decade of this century the campaign against child labor was being pushed vigorously at the state and national levels. Today, as a result of laws affecting employment, as well as the attitude of management and labor, it is difficult for boys even at the age of seventeen to obtain many types of jobs. In European countries three quarters or more of the youth go to work at fourteen or fifteen years of age.

As a consequence of the changes in universities and colleges in the nineteenth century and the alteration of the employment situation since World War I, the American public high school has become an institution which has no counterpart in any other country. With few exceptions, for the most part in large eastern cities, the public high school is expected to provide education for *all* the youth living in a town, city, or district. Such a high school has become known as a "comprehensive" high school in contrast to the

"specialized" high schools which provide vocational education or which admit on a selective basis and offer only an
academic curriculum. The local factors which have determined, and still determine, some of the features of a comprehensive high school are discussed later in this report, as
are the pros and cons of the selective academic high school
and the specialized vocational school.

Thousands of comprehensive high schools of considerable size exist throughout the United States. Though gen-
eralization about American public education is highly
dangerous (and I shall avoid it as far as possible in this
report), I believe it accurate to state that a high school
accommodating all the youth of a community is typical
of American public education. I think it safe to say that
the comprehensive high school is characteristic of our society and further that it has come into being because of our
economic history and our devotion to the ideals of equality
of opportunity and equality of status.

It is hardly necessary to say that a European finds the
educational tasks facing the teachers and administrators of
a comprehensive high school almost beyond his comprehension. (But this is the case also with some Americans whose
children have not attended such a school.) Almost as incomprehensible as the American college and the American
high school is the characteristic arrangement in the United
States for managing our tax-supported schools. When one
tells a foreign visitor that we have tens of thousands of
local school boards with vast powers over the elementary
schools and the high schools, he is apt to say, "This is not a
system but a chaos." To which I always reply, "But it
works; most of us like it; and it appears to be as permanent a
feature of our society as most of our political institutions."
And then, in the hope of giving him some glimpse of the reasons why such an arrangement has developed and why, in
spite of its obvious drawbacks, it has so many friends, one
falls back again on history.

The doctrine of local responsibility and community independence can be related to our pioneer history without difficulty. Parish and county autonomy in the South, the seventeenth-century independence of New England church congregations, and suspicion of centralized government are among the factors that shaped the present political structure of our school systems in many states. Yet there is no uniform arrangement. To describe with any accuracy the methods of choosing school board members and the powers of the boards in the forty-eight states, one would have to have a truly encyclopedic memory for details. Since, however, the school boards, almost without exception, do have a great degree of freedom in managing the local school, I have addressed this report in the first instance to school board members. And since in many communities the school boards are elected, I venture to hope the report may be of interest to citizens committees concerned with public education. I have directed my attention mainly to the comprehensive high school. I hope the preceding paragraphs may, in part, answer the questions of any reader who, like some of my friends two years ago, wonders why I have chosen to study high schools and what I mean by the "comprehensive" high school. I trust I have provided at least a clue to my belief in the significance of a unique American educational institution and the importance of supporting and improving thousands of examples of this institution throughout the United States.

SECTION II

A Unique Feature:
The Comprehensive High School

As everyone directly concerned with American secondary education is well aware, there are a number of different types of high schools in the United States. In the first place, in many school systems the arrangement is what is known as a "6–3–3" system, in which a junior high school of three years plays an intermediary role between the elementary school and the senior high school of three years. In the older pattern, a senior high school course of four years follows eight years of an elementary school. I shall not attempt to pass judgment on the relative advantages of the 6–3–3 and 8–4 schemes or on certain variants of these two patterns which are also found in the United States. It would appear that in some communities, for historical and geographic reasons, the existence of two or more junior high schools sending students to the senior high school with a three-year course has advantages. Even in those systems in which there is a junior high school, it is customary to regard grades nine through twelve as a unit, from the point of view of scheduling the students' work and arranging programs. Indeed, one finds that it is common practice in a three-year senior high school to consider the tenth grade as the sophomore class, although this group of boys and girls have only just entered the high school in question.

Leaving aside the differences between the three-year

and the four-year senior high schools, we can conveniently divide all the high schools in the United States into two general categories. In the one category are the specialized high schools found in certain large cities and, in the other, the comprehensive high schools, which are found in communities of all sizes. The specialized high school offers a program adapted to a special group of students and usually requires evidence of certain aptitudes on the part of candidates for admission. For example, there is a specialized high school in New York City called The Bronx High School of Science. The Central High School in Philadelphia, which is usually spoken of as an "academic" or "college-preparatory" school, and the six-year Boston Latin School are other examples of specialized high schools which have entrance requirements and whose programs are of a strictly academic nature. Finally, one should mention among the specialized high schools the vocational high schools which are located in many cities along the Atlantic Coast and in a few of the large midwestern cities. These schools are also to be found in smaller communities in a few states in which federal funds provided under the Smith–Hughes Act of 1917 and such supplemental acts as the George–Barden Act of 1946 have been used by state authorities to develop separate vocational schools.

Limitations on the Comprehensiveness of a High School

I have already defined the comprehensive high school as a high school whose programs correspond to the educational needs of *all* the youth of the community. In those cities in which there are specialized high schools, particularly vocational schools, it may well happen that some of the boys and girls who reside in the district served by a comprehensive high school attend the specialized school, and to this degree the breadth of the program in the comprehensive high school is limited. Likewise, in those states in which separate vocational schools have been developed and supported, the comprehensive high school will not have among its programs the vocational offerings supported by federal funds. One can therefore speak of the "degree of comprehensiveness" of a high school.

As will be pointed out more than once in the course of this report, there are high schools whose comprehensiveness is limited not by the existence of a specialized high school, but by lack of interest in the community in certain types of programs which develop special skills immediately useful upon graduation. High schools whose comprehensiveness is thus limited by the nature of the community are to be found particularly in suburban areas and in high-income residential sections of large cities. In these schools one finds that the vast majority of boys and girls desire to enter a four-year college or university, largely because of the collegiate ambitions of parents. In such schools, one will find that courses in stenography, auto mechanics, mechanical drawing, or the building trades are either not offered or are elected by very few students.

Focus of the Present Study

I decided early to concentrate my attention primarily on high schools with a high degree of comprehensiveness. In these schools, more than half the students terminate their full-time education at graduation, and therefore a variety of vocational programs are offered. Programs are also available for those who have high academic ability. In such schools the administrators usually have as one of their objectives the development of a democratic school spirit and an understanding between students with different intellectual abilities and different vocational goals. I decided to concentrate my attention on the educational situation in the twenty-six states listed in Appendix A. I have personally visited one or more schools in most of them, a total of fifty-five in 18 of the more populous states. Except for one or two visits to observe certain special arrangements, I have not included the big cities. As noted above, the high schools in many of these cities are not fully comprehensive because of the existence of vocational schools, specialized academic high schools, or both. High schools with strong vocational programs and in which a majority of the boys and girls terminate their education on graduation are rarely to be found in suburban areas. Therefore, I have visited only a few suburban schools, although, thanks to my staff, I am well acquainted with the intimate details of a number of such schools. I early became convinced that a high school must have a graduating class of at least one hundred to function adequately as a comprehensive school. With few exceptions, the schools I chose to visit were therefore schools with a graduating class of considerably more than one hundred. The schools were located for the most part outside metropolitan areas in cities with populations between 10,000 and 100,000. (For a list of the schools visited, see Appendix B.)

The Question to Be Answered

As I indicated in Section I of this report, the comprehensive high school is an American development of this century. It has no equivalent, so far as I am aware, in any European country. If the high school is of sufficient size and located in a community where parental pressure for preparing for college is not overriding, those boys and girls who desire to pursue education beyond the high school level will be in a minority. The question arises whether, being in a minority, such students can obtain an adequate education. Stating it another way, one can raise the question whether, under one roof and under the same management, it is possible for a school to fulfill satisfactorily three functions: Can a school at one and the same time provide a good general education for *all* the pupils as future citizens of a democracy, provide elective programs for the majority to develop useful skills, and educate adequately those with a talent for handling advanced academic subjects—particularly foreign languages and advanced mathematics? The answer to this question would seem to be of considerable importance for the future of American education. If the answer were clearly in the negative, then a radical change in the structure of American public secondary education would be in order. If the students in a given geographic area who have the ability to profit from the study of foreign languages and advanced mathematics on the high school level cannot obtain an adequate education in a comprehensive high school, then one can argue that separate high schools for these students should be maintained, as is now the case in some of the large eastern cities. On the other hand, if the answer is in the affirmative, then no radical change in the basic pattern of American education would seem to be required.

The problem of protecting the interest, so to speak, of a minority in an institution arises not only in connection with the pupils who are scholastically able, but also in many schools in connection with the education of those boys who desire to make progress in learning a skilled trade during the high school years. A generation and more ago, in certain states those who were urging the expansion of vocational education with the aid of federal funds decided that it was impossible to do justice to the needs of boys desiring a vocational education within the framework of a general high school. In these states the administrators of the vocational funds insisted on setting up separate vocational schools or, at least, were lukewarm in their enthusiasm for vocational programs in the comprehensive high school. Knowing of this situation, I was curious to discover not only whether in a comprehensive high school the interests of the minority who are academically able were well protected, but also whether it was possible for such a school to provide a satisfactory program for developing certain vocational skills through shopwork if the state permitted the use of federal funds in the comprehensive high school.

A Cautionary Note

It is important to point out that this report is in no sense a survey of the comprehensive high school. The study has made no attempt to answer such questions as "How satisfactory is the typical American high school?" Indeed, I am now convinced that it is impossible to obtain information on which one could generalize about the success or failure of the American high school in regard to the education of any group of children. There are too many high schools of too many different types, and I doubt if any procedure can be worked out by which a meaningful sample can be drawn from the 21,000 public high schools. Unless some sort of valid sampling procedure were developed or one had large resources, it would be impossible even to pass judgment on the thousands of high schools of sufficient size in the twenty-six states which have been included in this study. As will be made evident by this report, however, it is possible to make valid judgments about American secondary education, but only *school by school*.

An Examination of Comprehensive High Schools in Eighteen States

To repeat, the three main objectives of a comprehensive high school are: *first*, to provide a general education for all the future citizens; *second*, to provide good elective programs for those who wish to use their acquired skills immediately on graduation; *third*, to provide satisfactory programs for those whose vocations will depend on their subsequent education in a college or university. If one could find a single comprehensive high school in the United States in which all three objectives were reached in a highly satisfactory manner, such a school might be taken as a model or pattern. Furthermore, unless there were some especially favorable local features which enabled such a school to attain these three objectives, the characteristics found might be developed in all the other schools of sufficient size in the United States.

Since state and regional differences do play some role in this vast country, I decided that I should attempt to locate satisfactory comprehensive high schools in different sections of the nation. To this end, I inquired through various sources as to the comprehensive high schools outside the metropolitan areas which had the reputation of doing a good job in providing education for students with a wide range of vocational interests and abilities. I specified that these schools should be of such a nature that less than half the boys and girls were going on to college and the distribution of academic ability roughly corresponded to the national norm (median I.Q. 100–105). Not more than three or four in each state were picked from a list of several dozen. There may well have been many better schools in each section of the country, for our visits were limited, in part, by travel arrangements.

In my visits to the schools, I was accompanied by one or two members of my staff. In advance of the visit, communication with the superintendent and principal had established a rough outline of the schedule we wished to follow, and I had obtained a certain amount of statistical information about the school. In each school, in addition to the discussion with the superintendent and principal, we met teachers of each of the academic subjects in small groups for a fifteen- to twenty-minute conference, usually visited one or more classes (particularly in English and social studies), talked at some length with the leading members of the counseling staff, visited vocational shops, and finally met with about twenty of the student leaders. Whenever possible we conferred with one or more school board members. As a rule, the meetings with the teachers and the students were so arranged that the administrative officers were not present; the discussions were frank and the answers to the questions we raised were most helpful. I believe I obtained considerable insight into the school by our conversations with the student leaders. Somewhat to my surprise, I found that almost without exception those students elected to the student council or as officers of the class were in the group of the more academically able students who were preparing to go on to college. Such was the case in each of these schools, although the reader must remember that this collegebound group was always in the minority.

Criteria for Evaluating a Comprehensive High School

After visiting a number of schools, with the assistance of my staff I drew up a tentative list of criteria which would be useful in passing judgment on whether or not a given school was performing satisfactorily the three main functions of a comprehensive high school. In addition, I noted several features of school organization, the absence or presence of which seemed to me significant. A tentative list thus prepared was subjected to scrutiny by a number of experienced public school administrators, who made certain suggestions for improvement. As finally adopted, the list was as follows, and in all my reports I attempted to answer with a *yes* or *no* the questions implicit in the points listed:

A Check List to Assist in Evaluating a Comprehensive High School

A. Adequacy of general education for all as judged by:
 1. Offerings in English and American literature and composition
 2. Social studies, including American history
 3. Ability grouping in required courses
B. Adequacy of nonacademic elective program as judged by:
 4. The vocational programs for boys and commercial programs for girls
 5. Opportunities for supervised work experience
 6. Special provisions for very slow readers
C. Special arrangements for the academically talented students:
 7. Special provisions for challenging the highly gifted
 8. Special instruction in developing reading skills
 9. Summer sessions from which able students may profit
 10. Individualized programs (absence of tracks or rigid programs)
 11. School day organized into seven or more instructional periods
D. Other features:
 12. Adequacy of the guidance service
 13. Student morale
 14. Well-organized homerooms
 15. The success of the school in promoting an understanding between students with widely different academic abil-

ities and vocational goals (effective social interaction among students).

(More details of my procedures in judging these fifteen items are given in Appendix C.)

In addition to attempting to evaluate each school in terms of the fifteen points listed above, I was concerned with the instruction in mathematics, science, and foreign languages. Discussions with teachers of these subjects, visits to classrooms, and the comments of students threw light on the adequacy of the offerings and often on the effectiveness of the teaching. It was clear from what the teachers said that only a fraction of the boys and girls in the school in question were able to study effectively and rewardingly a wide program of advanced mathematics, science, and foreign languages. I refer to these students as the "academically talented." In a school in which the distribution of academic talent corresponded roughly to the national norm, only about 15 to 20 per cent of the student body in the ninth grade seemed to be in this group. And it was evident that, in schools with an adequate counseling staff, a majority of the more able students could usually be spotted at least by the end of the eighth grade on the basis of aptitude tests of one sort or another, the records of their work in the lower grades, and teacher evaluations. There are undoubtedly some in the next 10 or 15 per cent who also have the ability to study effectively and rewardingly both foreign languages and mathematics, but the number of those who have real difficulty with either languages or mathematics seems to increase as over-all scholastic aptitude diminishes.

As I discussed with teachers and guidance officers the work of the more able students, I became more and more interested in the programs of the academically talented. Yet, in no school which I visited was it possible for the administrator or the counseling officer to answer with assurance the following question: Are all the able students (say the top 15 or 20 per cent) in this high school electing the twelfth-grade mathematics course (often trigonometry) and the physics course, usually offered in the twelfth grade? Questions of this type which could also be asked about the foreign language program could only be answered in general terms based on an opinion formed by the counselors, the administrators, and the teachers. Information of this sort is obviously of the greatest importance in judging the school under investigation; it might easily happen that the vocational programs leading to the development of skills marketable on graduation would be so attractive as to draw into the programs students who had very high aptitude for academic work. Or even if these programs were not attractive, it might be that the bright-but-lazy boy or girl would concentrate attention on subjects which do not require homework, such as art and music, or typing, or shopwork, rather than elect a stiff academic program.

Because I was unable to obtain from my visits even an approximate answer to the questions about the programs of the more able students, I decided to ask the principals of twenty-two of the schools if they would provide me with what I called an "academic inventory."

I wish to record here my indebtedness to those who cooperated in providing this information at no inconsiderable trouble to themselves. What I asked was to have a list prepared of the students graduated in 1957 whose academic abilities would have placed them in the top 25 per cent of their class prior to the ninth grade. The selection, I suggested, should be made on the basis of a scholastic aptitude test or series of tests. I asked for the full four-year program of each of the students on such a list, omitting the student's name, of course, and indicating whether the student was a boy or girl. From these programs it was then possible for me to answer a variety of questions concerning what courses were being elected by those who were the most able from the point of view of handling academic subjects. In working over the information supplied by the schools, I decided to summarize the programs of the 15 per cent of the most academically able on a national basis as measured by the test scores given us by the school; I would thus have at hand information about the programs of the academically talented. It was evident that the programs of the boys and girls should be treated separately, as there was a clear difference in most schools between programs chosen by boys and those elected by girls.

Principal Findings of My Study

The question I set out to answer I can now answer in the affirmative. *I found eight schools which, in my judgment, were satisfactorily fulfilling the three main objectives of a comprehensive high school.* They were offering adequate instruction in English and social studies as part of general education required of all. These schools were providing significant nonacademic programs which were elected by a substantial number of students. In these same schools, the academic inventory showed that more than half the academically talented boys had studied at least seven years of mathematics and science as well as seven years of English and social studies. This fact is interesting in view of the recent stress on mathematics and science. (I shall report a few pages later on the quality of instruction.) On the other hand, in no school had a majority of the academically talented girls studied as much as seven years of mathematics and science.

The situation with regard to the study of foreign languages in these eight schools was, in most cases, not satisfactory. In only two schools had a majority of the academically talented boys studied foreign language for as long as three years. In most schools, even the few who had elected to study foreign languages for three or four years had to be content with two years of one language and one or two of another. The academic inventory showed a somewhat better picture so far as the academically talented girls were concerned: in five schools a majority of these girls had studied foreign language for three or more years.

A little arithmetic makes it clear that in those schools in which a majority of the academically talented boys had studied seven years of English and social studies, as well as three years of foreign languages and seven years of mathematics and science, a total of seventeen academic courses with homework had been taken in four years. In only one of the eight schools was this the case for the academically talented boys, and in no school was it the case for the girls.

In all but a few of the schools I have visited, the majority of bright boys and girls were not working hard enough. Academic studies did not cover a wide enough range. Both these deficiencies in the majority of schools on which I have information can be readily corrected by a shift of emphasis on the part of those in charge. Improvement would come about almost automatically in most schools if seven years of English and social studies were required and if, instead of a two-year course in a foreign language, a sequence of four years of at least one foreign language were offered, provided the counselors emphasized the importance of foreign language for the academically talented boys and mathematics and science for the academically talented girls.

Table 1 on page 24 summarizes my conclusions about each of the twenty-two schools visited from which we obtained an academic inventory. These conclusions are based

School* Size of Graduating Class	A 95	B 373	C 760	D 407	E 273
SCHOOL SUMMARY					
▶ Adequacy of General Education for all as judged by:					
1. Adequate instruction in English Composition	X	X		X	X
2. Adequate instruction in Social Studies	X			X	X
3. In required subjects, students grouped by ability	X	X	X	X	X
▶ Adequacy of Nonacademic Elective Program as judged by:					
4. Adequate Nonacademic Elective Programs	X		X	X	
5. Adequate opportunities for supervised Work Experience	X		X	X	
6. Special Provision for Slow Readers	X		X	X	X
▶ Special Arrangements for the academically talented student:					
7. Special provisions for challenging the highly gifted		X	X	X	X
8. Special instruction in developing Reading Skills	X			X	
9. Regular Summer Session				X	
10. Individualized Programs	X	X		X	X
11. School day organized into 7 or more instruction periods	X	X	X	X	X
▶ Other Features					
12. Guidance Service	X	X	X	X	X
13. Good Student Morale	X	X	X	X	X
14. Well-organized Homerooms		X			
15. Effective Social Interaction among students		X		X	X
ACADEMIC INVENTORY					
16. A majority of the academically talented boys in their four high school years took at least:					
a. 7 years of Math and Science	X	X	X	X	X
b. 7 years of English and Social Studies	X	X	X	X	
c. 3 years of Foreign Languages	X	X	X		X
d. 17 full academic subjects	X	X	X	X	X
17. A majority of the academically talented girls in their four high school years took at least:					
a. 7 years of Math and Science					
b. 7 years of English and Social Studies	X		X	X	
c. 3 years of Foreign Languages	X	X	X	X	X
d. 17 full academic subjects	X	X	X		X

* These 22 high schools are located in the East, Middle West, Southwest, and Far West.

(X indicates fulfillment of the criterion)

| F | G | H | I | J | K | L | M | N | O | P | Q | R | S | T | U | V |
596	175	443	422	350	378	400	312	550	73	100	382	440	310	502	390	797
X		X	X	X			X	X			X	X		X		
X	X	X	X	X	X		X	X			X			X	X	X
X			X		X		X					X		X	X	X
X	X	X	X	X			X	X	X	X**	X**		X		X	X	X
X		X	X				X	X		X					X	
X			X		X	X	X					X				X
X	X	X	X		X	X	X		X				X	X	X	X
		X	X	X					X				X			X
			X		X			X				X				X
X	X	X	X	X	X		X	X	X			X	X		X	X
X	X		X	X				X								
	X		X	X	X	X	X		X	X		X	X	X		X
X	X	X	X	X	X	X	X	X	X	X	X	X	X		X	X
	X	X		X	X	X	X				X					
	X	X	X	X	X	X		X	X	X	X		X			
X	X	X	X	X	X	X	X	X		X	X	X	X			X
X		X			X	X	X	X	X	X	X			X		
X			X													
	X	X							X			X				
X	X	X	X	X	X	X	X	X	X	X	X	X	X			X
X					X		X	X					X	X		

** Schools O and P are Rural Consolidated High Schools. They have limited vocational trade and industrial programs but have strong programs in agriculture.

on the check list, given on pages 19–20, and the academic inventory. A more detailed description of the criteria corresponding to each of the items in Table 1 is given in Appendix C, and two tables which provide further information from the academic inventories of these schools are given in Appendix D. The eight schools already mentioned which I believe were providing satisfactory general education (Items 1, 2, 16b, and 17b in Table 1), satisfactory nonacademic electives (Item 4), and in which a majority of the academically talented boys in the class of 1957 had studied seven years of mathematics and science (Item 16a) are A, D, F, H, J, M, N, and P. In all but two of these schools, I found significant work experience programs (Item 5) and, in four, special provisions for the slow reader (Item 6). Half of the number used ability grouping (Item 3), and the same number (but not all the same schools) had special provisions for challenging the highly gifted (Item 7). In all but one school there were no clear-cut tracks or labeled programs; on the contrary, the programs of the students were on an individualized basis (Item 10). The guidance (Item 12) in five of the eight I judged to be satisfactory. Summer sessions (Item 9) for the able as well as the slow students were in successful operation in three of these schools, and I found developmental reading programs (Item 8) in three of these eight schools.

In all eight schools which met the test of adequacy on the points of general education, nonacademic elective programs, and the mathematical and scientific programs of a majority of the academically talented boys, I judged student morale to be high (Item 13). And in five of these schools, it seemed that there was a significant interaction between students of different abilities and vocational goals (Item 15); three of the schools had well-organized homerooms (Item 14). I was impressed with the success of the homeroom in promoting an understanding between students of different vocational aims. One of the highly important objectives of a good comprehensive high school is surely developing a democratic spirit.

Four of the schools were organized with seven or more periods in the day (Item 11). The significance of the seven-period or eight-period day in terms of the election of art and music by the academically talented can be seen by an inspection of Appendix D, in which the findings are discussed in more detail. If a school is organized with a sufficient number of periods in a day, there is no difficulty in having the programs of the academically talented include as many as four years of art, music, and other electives, as well as five subjects with homework in each of the four years (twenty academic subjects with homework).

It will be noted from Item 16d, Table 1 that in a total of nine schools the programs of a majority of the academically talented boys included at least seventeen academic subjects with homework; indeed, in two, a majority of the same boys had studied at least eighteen subjects in four years. (The data are given in Appendix D.) Yet, because in six of these nine schools I had some questions about the adequacy of either the general or the vocational programs, I have not included them in the group of schools judged satisfactory on the three counts listed above. If one leaves aside these two evaluations, obviously only an approximation to a solidly based judgment, the picture in terms of the academic inventory appears quite different. Not in three but in eight of the twenty-two schools were a majority of the academically talented boys studying seventeen subjects with homework, including seven years of mathematics and science. However, a moment's reflection makes it plain that this difference has no significance for an over-all appraisal of the high schools of the United States. My sampling of schools was far from random in the first place,

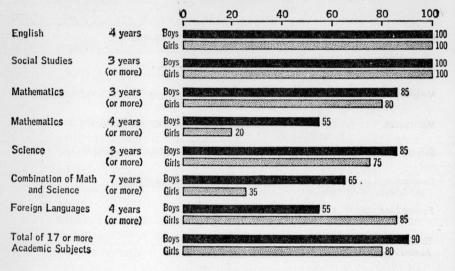

SCHOOL C

Per Cent of Academically Talented Studying Subjects Listed

Subject	Duration	Group	Per Cent
English	4 years	Boys	100
		Girls	100
Social Studies	3 years (or more)	Boys	100
		Girls	100
Mathematics	3 years (or more)	Boys	85
		Girls	80
Mathematics	4 years (or more)	Boys	55
		Girls	20
Science	3 years (or more)	Boys	85
		Girls	75
Combination of Math and Science	7 years (or more)	Boys	65 .
		Girls	35
Foreign Languages	4 years (or more)	Boys	55
		Girls	85
Total of 17 or more Academic Subjects		Boys	90
		Girls	80

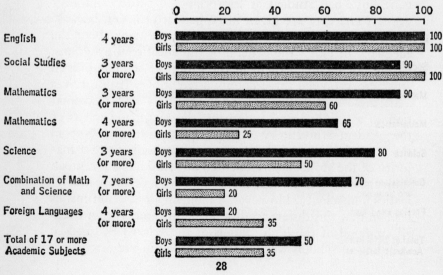

SCHOOL D

Per Cent of Academically Talented Studying Subjects Listed

Subject	Duration	Group	Per Cent
English	4 years	Boys	100
		Girls	100
Social Studies	3 years (or more)	Boys	90
		Girls	100
Mathematics	3 years (or more)	Boys	90
		Girls	60
Mathematics	4 years (or more)	Boys	65
		Girls	25
Science	3 years (or more)	Boys	80
		Girls	50
Combination of Math and Science	7 years (or more)	Boys	70
		Girls	20
Foreign Languages	4 years (or more)	Boys	20
		Girls	35
Total of 17 or more Academic Subjects		Boys	50
		Girls	35

28

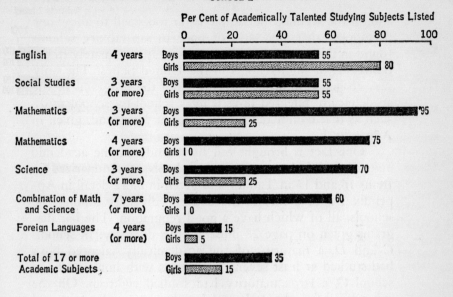

SCHOOL 1

Per Cent of Academically Talented Studying Subjects Listed

			0	20	40	60	80	100
English	4 years	Boys				55		
		Girls					80	
Social Studies	3 years (or more)	Boys				55		
		Girls				55		
Mathematics	3 years (or more)	Boys						95
		Girls	25					
Mathematics	4 years (or more)	Boys					75	
		Girls	0					
Science	3 years (or more)	Boys				70		
		Girls	25					
Combination of Math and Science	7 years (or more)	Boys				60		
		Girls	0					
Foreign Languages	4 years (or more)	Boys	15					
		Girls	5					
Total of 17 or more Academic Subjects		Boys	35					
		Girls	15					

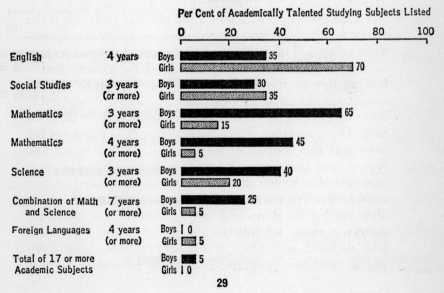

SCHOOL V

Per Cent of Academically Talented Studying Subjects Listed

			0	20	40	60	80	100
English	4 years	Boys	35					
		Girls				70		
Social Studies	3 years (or more)	Boys	30					
		Girls	35					
Mathematics	3 years (or more)	Boys				65		
		Girls	15					
Mathematics	4 years (or more)	Boys		45				
		Girls	5					
Science	3 years (or more)	Boys		40				
		Girls	20					
Combination of Math and Science	7 years (or more)	Boys	25					
		Girls	5					
Foreign Languages	4 years (or more)	Boys	0					
		Girls	5					
Total of 17 or more Academic Subjects		Boys	5					
		Girls	0					

29

and, in the second, the sample is far too small to allow one to suppose that any ratio of poor to satisfactory schools found in this group would apply even approximately to the thousands of high schools in the United States. The only way to get significant statistics about the programs of the academically talented boys is by a school-by-school study such as that completed by the state of Maryland, given in Appendix E.

One fact is brought out by a study of the academic inventories of the twenty-two schools as summarized in Items 16 and 17 in Table 1 and given in more detail in Appendix D. This fact is the extreme diversity among the schools, all of which have a good reputation. The bar diagrams given on page 28 illustrate this diversity. In schools *C* and *D*, a majority of the academically talented boys had studied at least seventeen courses with homework. In school *C*, a large majority had studied eighteen. On the other hand, in schools *V* and *I* such was not the case, and in both schools English was neglected by the boys.

One matter on which I should also like to report is the extent to which I found the nonacademic elective programs to be composed of meaningful sequences of courses leading to the development of marketable skills, rather than a hodgepodge of miscellaneous subjects. I venture to take some space to consider this point, because a considerable body of criticism of our public schools has been directed to it. There are those who believe the work in the shops for boys and the courses in stenography, clerical machines, typing, and home economics for girls have no place in a high school in which academic subjects are studied by any considerable fraction of the student body. My conclusion after visiting the shops and talking with the vocational directors in many schools is quite the contrary. There is a false antithesis sometimes drawn between vocational work and an academic program. Even those who elect a voca-

CAREER COMMITMENT DIAGRAMS

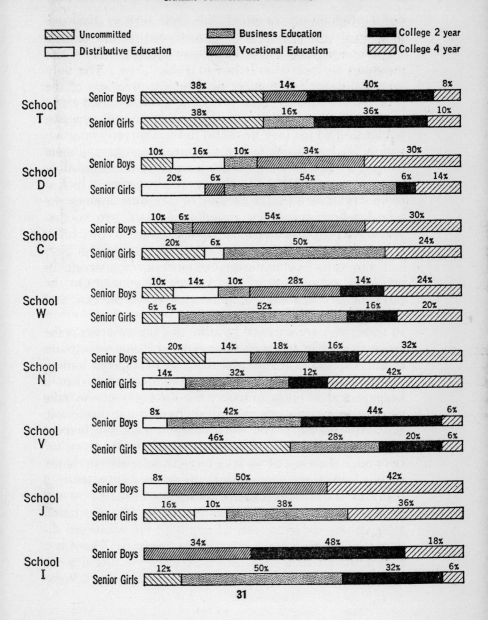

Uncommitted | Business Education | College 2 year
Distributive Education | Vocational Education | College 4 year

School T
Senior Boys: 38% | 14% | 40% | 8%
Senior Girls: 38% | 16% | 36% | 10%

School D
Senior Boys: 10% | 16% | 10% | 34% | 30%
Senior Girls: 20% | 6% | 54% | 6% | 14%

School C
Senior Boys: 10% | 6% | 54% | 30%
Senior Girls: 20% | 6% | 50% | 24%

School W
Senior Boys: 10% | 14% | 10% | 28% | 14% | 24%
Senior Girls: 6% | 6% | 52% | 16% | 20%

School N
Senior Boys: 20% | 14% | 18% | 16% | 32%
Senior Girls: 14% | 32% | 12% | 42%

School V
Senior Boys: 8% | 42% | 44% | 6%
Senior Girls: 46% | 28% | 20% | 6%

School J
Senior Boys: 8% | 50% | 42%
Senior Girls: 16% | 10% | 38% | 36%

School I
Senior Boys: 34% | 48% | 18%
Senior Girls: 12% | 50% | 32% | 6%

31

tional program are devoting half their time to academic work in English, social studies, mathematics, and science.

Not only have I found adequate nonacademic elective programs as reported in Item 4 in Table 1, but I have been surprised to see in a number of schools to what a high degree the students in these programs are committed to an elective sequence which is aimed toward developing a particular skill which may be useful to them directly on graduation. Such students, it seems to me, have a commitment to their studies which gives them an attitude toward their whole program, including the required courses, which is more serious than that of the boy or girl of medium ability who has been forced by an ambitious parent to take an academic program and who is failing or barely passing courses in foreign languages, mathematics, and science.

The career commitment diagrams that appear on the preceding page illustrate the degree of commitment of boys and girls in 8 schools, by no means exceptional among those visited. On the diagrams the word *vocational* refers to those who are enrolled in a Smith–Hughes program or its equivalent in terms of the amount of time devoted to shopwork; *business* refers to courses in typing, stenography, and the use of clerical machines or courses in bookkeeping and business practice; the *distributive* education programs involve work in retail shops on a part-time basis. (See Appendix F.) The word *college* on the diagrams, it must be remembered, refers to the goal the students had in mind; it does *not* necessarily mean that the students were enrolled in a separate college-preparatory program. In many of the schools, there were no such clear-cut tracks or programs.

Evidence in Regard to the Quality
of the Teaching of Mathematics and Science

The schools from which we obtained an academic inventory appeared to me almost without exception to be offering satisfactory courses in twelfth-grade mathematics and physics. However, I had no basis on which to answer such questions as this: Is the instruction in these subjects as good as the teaching in schools of good reputation from which a vast majority of the graduating class go on to college? In order to obtain evidence on this point, I arranged to have tests in trigonometry and physics given to the students in these subjects in thirteen comprehensive high schools and in four well-known public high schools located in or near large cities in the East, the Midwest, and on the Pacific Coast, which I shall designate as the "control" schools. These control schools are of acknowledged excellence and send a large number of graduates to four-year colleges.

It is obvious that for a meaningful comparison of the instruction offered one must measure the performance on achievement tests of students of comparable ability. A moment's reflection makes it evident that one could not expect a class of dull pupils to do as well on a test of trigonometry, for example, as a class of bright pupils even if, in both instances, equally able teachers had provided the instruction. This point, by the way, is often overlooked by laymen who judge a school by the degree of success of its students on some national examination without taking into account differences in the ability of students from school to school and from year to year within a school. A new test called "School and College Ability Test" (SCAT) has been recently developed by the Educational Testing Service. This test provides a measure of "the capacity of a student to undertake academic work of the next higher level of schooling." It measures the two kinds of school-related abilities which are most important in the greatest number of school and college endeavors: verbal (SCAT–V) and quantitative (SCAT–Q). This test was taken by the same students who took the achievement tests in trigonometry and physics. The achievement tests used were the Cooperative Trigonometry Test and the College Entrance Examination Board Physics Test. Both are considered to be tests which measure mastery of those aspects of the subjects

TABLE 2: *Physics Test Results for Boys at Three Levels of Quantitative Ability*

Ability Level	Type of School	SCAT-Q Score Range of School Means	Physics Score Range of School Means
High	Control	331–333	564–609
	Comprehensive	329–334	502–692
Medium	Control	319–320	506–598
	Comprehensive	318–320	459–568
Low	Control	303–309	474–535
	Comprehensive	294–307	417–513

TABLE 3: *Trigonometry Test Results for Boys at Three Levels of Quantitative Ability*

Ability Level	Type of School	SCAT-Q Score Range of School Means	Trigonometry Score Range of School Means
High	Control	329–334	55.2–66.9
	Comprehensive	326–334	54.1–66.7
Medium	Control	319–321	52.7–60.0
	Comprehensive	319–321	47.5–61.2
Low	Control	304–309	46.8–57.9
	Comprehensive	299–313	44.9–58.7

in question which educators agree should be a part of the syllabus in every school.

The results of these tests can be summed up in a few words. There was no important difference, as revealed by these tests, in the degree of mastery of trigonometry and physics by the students tested in the comprehensive high schools and those in the four control high schools. The preceding tables (Tables 2 and 3) summarize the important findings. Since the number of girls in the physics and trigonometry classes was small in most of the comprehensive schools, only the results obtained by testing the boys have been included in the tables. The inclusion of the girls or a separate comparison of the results of the girls would not have altered the conclusions.

In order to compare groups with similar ability to handle quantitative problems, the boys in each school were assigned to three groups. The first subsample, or the high-ability group, consisted of all boys who answered correctly at least forty-six out of fifty questions on SCAT–Q, the second consisted of all those who answered correctly between forty-one and forty-five questions, and the third consisted of all those who answered correctly forty or less. This particular grouping was chosen because it provided reasonably large groups of comparable ability. It would have been possible to obtain more homogeneous groups by reducing the range of scores, but the number of students in each group would have been so small as to produce statistics with an unreasonably large sampling error.

The test performance of boys who studied physics is summarized in Table 2. In the high-ability group the mean scores in physics ranged between 564 and 609. In the thirteen comprehensive schools, students of similar ability had mean physics scores ranging between 502 and 692. There is clearly a good deal of overlap between the ranges of achievement of superior students in the two types of school.

The results for the middle-ability groups also show an overlap, although there is some difference in favor of the control schools.

The ranges of means on SCAT–Q for the low group indicate a marked difference between the low-scoring student in the two types of school: the poorer students in the control schools are more able than the poorer students in the comprehensive schools. Even though the students in this low group are not well matched in ability, there is some overlap in achievement in physics.

It should be borne in mind that these so-called high-, middle-, and low-ability groups are quite able students. The publisher's norms show that the average student in the high-ability group is in the top 1 per cent of a cross section of public high school seniors, the average student in the middle group is at the ninety-third percentile, and the average student in the low-ability group even for comprehensive high schools—the least able subsample of all—is at the eighty-second percentile.

The scores on the physics test indicate a high level of competence in the subject. The score 500 is the expected score for a twelfth grader whose mathematical ability has been estimated to be at approximately the seventy-fifth percentile among twelfth-graders throughout the nation. Many of the means in Table 2 are far above 500.

Table 3 presents data for boys taking trigonometry. The results are similar to those presented in Table 2 for boys taking physics. There is considerable overlap between the ranges of achievement-test means for students of similar ability from the two types of schools.

An interesting fact that emerges from a study of the detailed results is that students in *one* of the comprehensive schools, when their aptitudes are taken into account, achieved better in both trigonometry and physics than did the students in any of the four control schools.

Elimination of the Small High School— A Top Priority

Most of the schools visited by me and my staff during this past year have had graduating classes of one hundred or more. From what I observed in these schools, in the two schools noted in Table 1 with graduating classes of less than one hundred, and in a much smaller school I visited, I am convinced small high schools can be satisfactory only at exorbitant expense. The truth of this statement is evident if one considers the distribution of academic talent in the school which serves all the youth of the community. It will be a rare district where more than 25 per cent of a high school class can study with profit twelfth-grade mathematics, physics, and a foreign language for four years (assuming that standards are maintained). If a school has a twelfth grade of only forty and if indeed only a quarter of the group can handle the advanced subjects effectively, instruction in mathematics, science, and foreign languages would have to be provided for a maximum of ten students. If the girls shy away from the mathematics and science as they do in most of the schools I visited, the twelfth-grade mathematics classes may be as small as six or seven. To provide adequate teachers for specialized subjects is extremely expensive. Furthermore, to maintain an interest in academic subjects among a small number is not always easy. Wide academic programs are not likely to be offered when the academically talented in a school are so few in number. The situation in regard to the nonacademic elective programs in a small high school is even worse. The capital outlay for equipment as well as the salaries of the special vocational instructors adds up to such a large figure in terms of the few enrolled as to make vocational programs almost prohibitively expensive in schools with a graduating class of less than one hundred.

For the reasons given in the preceding paragraph and elaborated in Section IV (p. 77), the district which supports a comprehensive high school must be large enough to provide a school of sufficient size. *I should like to record at this point my conviction that in many states the number one problem is the elimination of the small high school by district reorganization.* Such reorganization has been virtually accomplished by leadership at the state level, legislative action, and subsequent decisions of the electorate in a few states. In all others, citizens who wish to improve public education might well devote their energies to mobilizing opinion in behalf of district reorganization directed toward the reduction of the number of small high schools. (See Appendix G for statistics on the percentage of high schools in the United States which are too small.)

The Community and the School Board

There are three requisites for the successful operation of a high school: *first*, a school board composed of intelligent, honest, devoted citizens who understand that their function is policy-making and not administration; *second*, a first-rate superintendent; *third*, a good principal. Without a good school board the situation is almost hopeless. If members of a school board become involved in the appointment of teachers and in other matters of patronage, the maintenance of good morale in the teaching staff becomes almost impossible, however excellent may be the superintendent and the principal. Given a good school board and strong leadership by the superintendent and principal, an excellent group of teachers will be recruited, and it is hardly necessary to emphasize that on the quality of the teachers (assuming wise leadership) the quality of the education must ultimately depend.

Probably one of the most important factors in determining whether a high school is providing adequately for the education of the academically talented is the attitude of the community. Too much emphasis on basketball, football, and marching bands may affect the decisions of the school board, the administrators, and the teachers; and, often equally important, community activities may take up too much of the students' time.

In visiting a school even for so short a time as a day, one learns something about the community. I must admit that it was with considerable dismay that I observed the demands the communities often put upon high school youth for use of out-of-school hours. Talks with students were particularly revealing in this regard. I have been in some cities where boys and girls said that they were out of their homes after the evening dinner hour more often than they were in them. There was nothing wrong, per se, with what they were doing—club meetings, junior lodge meetings, dramatics and music rehearsals, athletic events sponsored by community organizations. But their home study time *was* interfered with. In fact, teachers frequently said that they could not hold students to home study because of community demands on student time and that, therefore, standards in courses fell. Yet in many schools, the ambitious, bright students told me that they felt they should be doing fifteen hours of homework a week.

Here it must be added that high schools themselves are sometimes offenders in this matter by not protecting the home study time of their students. It is not uncommon for schools to play basketball games on nights before school days and to close school early so that their boys and girls can attend games scheduled for the afternoon. Occasionally rehearsals for school events are held at night. If schools want to be in a strong position when they ask the community to respect the study time of their boys and girls, they should show that same respect themselves.

Conclusion

I can sum up my conclusions in a few sentences. The number of small high schools must be drastically reduced through district reorganization. Aside from this important change, I believe no radical alteration in the basic pattern of American education is necessary in order to improve our public high schools. If all the high schools were functioning as well as some I have visited, the education of all American youth would be satisfactory, except for the study of foreign languages and the guidance of the more able girls. Most of the schools which I found unsatisfactory in one or more respects could become satisfactory by relatively minor changes, though I have no doubt that there are schools even of sufficient size where major improvements in organization and instruction would be in order. If the fifty-five schools I have visited, all of which have a good reputation, are at all representative of American public high schools, I think one general criticism would be in order: The academically talented student, as a rule, is not being sufficiently challenged, does not work hard enough, and his program of academic subjects is not of sufficient range. The able boys too often specialize in mathematics and science to the exclusion of foreign languages and to the neglect of English and social studies. The able girls, on the other hand, too often avoid mathematics and science as well as the foreign languages. As I have indicated in the preceding paragraph, a correction of this situation in many instances will depend upon an altered attitude of the community quite as much as upon action by a school board or the school administration.

SECTION III

Recommendations for Improving
Public Secondary Education

Before presenting a number of specific recommendations
addressed to school board members and school administrators, a few words of explanation may be in order. My recommendations are based on what I have observed. Almost
without exception, I can point to one or more schools in
which the recommended type of organization or practice
can be found, not as an experiment but as something tried
and tested over a period of years. Taken together, they
outline the important characteristics of a satisfactory high
school which is widely comprehensive, and the recommendations must be judged as a whole, for some taken separately would be almost impossible to put into effect.

Because I have been interested in determining the characteristics of a satisfactory comprehensive high school, this
section of the report may appear too conservative for the
taste of many readers. Yet it follows from the premises of
my study that my recommendations would include only
what I had found to be well-established features of at least
one school. I have seen a number of interesting new departures, such as the use of television, which in my opinion
have not yet developed to a point where they can be regarded as firmly established features of a comprehensive
school. I hardly need emphasize the importance of experimentation and the desirability of innovation in all phases of

education. It would be most unfortunate if the conservative recommendations in this section, necessarily presented in rather dogmatic form, should lead anyone to believe I was in favor of freezing the development of the curriculum or the organization of a high school.

As a matter of fact, I can easily draw up a long list of urgent problems which can be solved only by schools trying out new ideas and then evaluating the new departures as carefully as possible. To mention only a few items, new areas of vocational work in electronics for boys appear to need exploration, and successful adventures in this field should be brought to the attention of all concerned with vocational education. I found widespread dissatisfaction with the course in world history. Furthermore, I found few teachers or administrators who were willing to endorse a four-year sequence in social studies because of their doubts as to the value of what would be taught the fourth year. Therefore, experimentation, evaluation, and discussion of the findings of social science teachers would seem to me to be high on the list of priorities in curriculum development. There is ferment in many areas of instruction: a new approach to physics is being rapidly developed; there are several new approaches to a four-year sequence of mathematics; foreign language teachers in some school systems are starting instruction in lower grades. If I had been engaged in passing judgment on the details of the content of courses, I think I should not have been able to assess any of these new developments. Time must tell which of them are successful. But one must rejoice at the evidence on all sides of a new spirit of examination of the high school curriculum. Undoubtedly new ideas about the organization of the school day and the allocation of time among various subjects should be tried out and tested as should the possibility of moving algebra as well as languages into the lower grades. Ten or even five years from now, at least some of my recommendations may need serious revision because of what has been demonstrated as successful practice. In short, there is no inconsistency between adapting the best from what has been well tried and tested and having an open mind about the outcome of experiment now planned or underway.

Some of the recommendations which follow would involve an increase in the budget and therefore require school board action; they would have to be explained to the community to receive support. These recommendations are of particular importance to the school boards and to the citizens to whom each school board is responsible. Other recommendations concern the details of school organization and curriculum; in the first instance, these recommendations belong in the province of the school administrators. I assume that if a school is functioning satisfactorily the relationship between the school board, the superintendent, and the principal will be such that changes introduced by the principal and superintendent will be fully explained to the school board which, in turn, can explain them to the public.

I should like at this point to restate my judgment, based upon months of traveling and visits to schools in eighteen states as well as upon discussions with many, many school administrators, that three things are necessary to have a good high school, provided that it is of sufficient size: *first*, a school board composed of devoted, intelligent, understanding citizens who realize fully the *distinction between policy making and administration; second*, a first-rate superintendent; and *third*, a good principal. I assume that the school board will leave the development of the curriculum to the administrative officers and the teaching staff but will be kept informed of all developments. Furthermore, the members will reserve the right to ask the superintendent, and through the superintendent the principal, searching questions about the details of the curriculum. They will not only reserve this right but exercise it from time to time.

One final word of warning addressed to school board members. Some of the recommendations listed below can be put into effect at the beginning of the school year without upsetting in any way the morale of the teaching staff. Other recommendations, however, can be effective only if a majority of the teachers are convinced of their wisdom. If an administrative officer feels that these recommendations should be introduced, his first task would be to examine the problems involved with committees of teachers and then persuade the teachers that the recommendations should be given a thorough trial. I have in mind particularly the controversial subject of ability grouping, any recommendations in regard to marking or grading, and the requirements for admission to advanced courses.

Recommendation 1: THE COUNSELING SYSTEM

In a satisfactory school system the counseling should start in the elementary school, and there should be good articulation between the counseling in the junior and senior high schools if the pattern is 6–3–3 or between the counseling in the elementary school and the high school if the system is organized on an 8–4 basis. There should be one full-time counselor (or guidance officer) for every two hundred fifty to three hundred pupils in the high school. The counselors should have had experience as teachers but should be devoting virtually full time to the counseling work; they should be familiar with the use of tests and measurements of the aptitudes and achievement of pupils. The function of the counselor is not to supplant the parents but to supplement parental advice to a youngster. To this end, the counselor should be in close touch with the parent as well as the pupil. Through consultation, an attempt should be made each year to work out an elective program for the student which corresponds to the student's interest and ability as determined by tests of scholastic aptitude, the recorded achievement as measured by grades in courses, and by teachers' estimates. The counselors should be sympathetic to the elective programs which develop marketable skills; they should also understand the program for the slow readers and be ready to cooperate with the teachers of this group of students.

In guiding the more able students, the counselor should be on the lookout for the bright boy or girl whose high ability has been demonstrated by the results of aptitude tests given from time to time but whose achievement, as measured by grades in courses, has been low. The problem of motivating such pupils is a difficult one. I should like to emphasize at this point the importance of recognizing fully the role of adequate motivation in determining the eventual success of any student.

The framework in which the counselor operates depends upon school policy. For example, the policy of the school in regard to the vocational programs should be such as to insure that these programs are *not* used as dumping grounds for those of low academic ability. Furthermore, it should be school policy that the counselor arrange a meaningful sequence of courses in the elective programs of all the pupils. In a comprehensive high school of the type I am considering, a meaningful sequence for a majority of the students would be a series of courses leading to the development of marketable skills (see Recommendation 7, p. 51). In Recommendation 9 (p. 57) I set forth what I believe should be the minimum program of the academically talented. In most of the schools I have visited, there was relatively little pressure on the part of parents to have less-than-average students take difficult subjects. More often the counselors' main task was to persuade parents that their bright offspring should elect such subjects as eleventh- and twelfth-grade mathematics, physics, and foreign languages. On the other hand, I am familiar with a number of schools where the situation is just reversed. (See Section IV, C, The Suburban High School, p. 91.)

My views about counseling and guidance are based not only on my observations in the fifty-five schools I visited, but also on a special report prepared for me by Dr. R. C. Lloyd, Special Assistant to the superintendent of the Baltimore, Maryland, Public Schools. He visited a variety of schools and talked with many guidance officers in the course of his investigations.

Recommendation 2: INDIVIDUALIZED PROGRAMS

It should be the policy of the school that every student has an individualized program; there would be no classification of students according to clearly defined and labeled programs or tracks such as "college-preparatory," "vocational," "commercial." In advising the student as to his elective program, the counselor will be guided by the minimum program recommended as a matter of school policy for the academically talented or by recommended sequences leading to the development of skills marketable on graduation. It will turn out that many students of similar ability and vocational interests will have almost identical programs, but a student who has elected an academic sequence may shift to a vocational sequence and vice versa. Furthermore, with individualized programs, the students themselves do not feel that they are labeled according to the program they have chosen in the ninth or tenth grade. If flexibility is combined with a declaration of policy in regard to the programs for the academically talented and if a good guidance service is available, the academic inventory should show results as satisfactory as the results in a school which has a clear-cut academic or college-preparatory track.

A feeling of prestige is apt to be attached to those who are enrolled in an academic program if the school is rigidly divided into groups with different programs; and there will be pressure from ambitious parents to have their children, irrespective of ability, enrolled in the college preparatory track. Such pressures are difficult to resist and may lead many students to attempt advanced mathematics, physics, and foreign language courses which they cannot handle. The reader will see from examining Item 10, Table 1 (p. 24) that in seventeen of the twenty-two schools listed the students' programs had been organized on an individual basis.

Recommendation 3: REQUIRED PROGRAMS FOR ALL

A. GENERAL EDUCATION   The requirements for graduation for all students should be as follows:

four years of English, three or four years of social studies—including two years of history (one of which should be American history) and a senior course in American problems or American government—one year of mathematics in the ninth grade (algebra or general mathematics), and at least one year of science in the ninth or tenth grade, which might well be biology or general physical science. By a year, I mean that a course is given five periods a week throughout the academic year or an equivalent amount of time. This academic program of general education involves nine or ten courses with homework to be taken in four years and occupies more than half the time of most students, whatever their elective programs.

B. THE ELECTIVE PROGRAM The other requirement for graduation should be successful completion of at least seven more courses, not including physical education. *All students should be urged to include art and music in their elective programs.* All students should be advised to have as the central core of their elective programs significant sequences of courses, either those leading to the development of a marketable skill or those of an academic nature.

C. STANDARDS FOR PASS AND FAILURE This recommendation is directed to the principal of the high school and involves the kind of policy with which a school board should not be directly concerned. In order to assist the counselors in their work of guiding the students into programs which the students can handle effectively, the teachers of the advanced academic *elective* courses—foreign languages, mathematics, and science—should be urged to maintain high standards. They should be told not to hesitate to fail a student who does not meet the minimum level of performance they judge necessary for a mastery of the subject in question. In other words, the work in the academic elective courses should be judged on a standard of performance so high that students who do not have the ability to handle the subjects are discouraged from electing these courses and prevented from continuing in the sequence. On the other hand, for the *required* courses another standard should be applied. Since these courses are required of all, irrespective of ability, a student may be given a passing grade if he has worked to full capacity whether or not a certain level of achievement has been reached. A series of examinations in English composition (Recommendation 6) should insure the development of a minimum skill in composition; an eleventh grade test in arithmetic followed by a remedial twelfth-grade course is likewise to be recommended.

Recommendation 4: ABILITY GROUPING

In the required subjects and those elected by students with a wide range of ability, the students should be grouped according to ability, subject by subject. For example, in English, American history, ninth-grade algebra, biology, and physical science, there should be at least three types of classes—one for the more able in the subject, another for the large group whose ability is about average, and another for the very slow readers who should be handled by special teachers. The middle group might be divided into two or three sections according to the students' abilities in the subject in question. This type of grouping is not to be confused with across-the-board grouping according to which a given student is placed in a particular section in *all* courses. Under the scheme here recommended, for example, a student may be in the top section in English but the middle section in history or ninth-grade algebra.

Ability grouping is a highly controversial subject among administrators and teachers. I have met competent teachers who argued vigorously for heterogeneous grouping in all classes—that is to say, they argued that students of widely different academic abilities and reading skills should be in the same class. Other teachers were equally certain that justice cannot be done to either the bright student or the slow reader if both receive instruction in the same class. Some of those who feel that heterogeneous grouping is a mistake advocate across-the-board grouping or tracking. Others advocate grouping the students according to their ability in the subject in question.

In those subjects elected by a relatively small fraction of the student body, such as advanced mathematics and twelfth-grade physics, something approaching ability grouping comes about as a consequence of the elective nature of these subjects. As a rule, few if any of the boys and girls in the bottom half of the class in terms of academic ability are bold enough to elect these courses. In some schools, the majority of the students in these courses come at least from the top 15 to 25 per cent. In a few schools the biology course was divided according to ability into two groups, and the teachers thought it would be much better if three groupings were available. To some degree, ability grouping in science courses may be a consequence of the proper labeling of different courses in the same subject. For example, a course labeled "biology" is more likely to be taken by the able and ambitious students than one labeled "life science," which will be taken by the less bright students.

Recommendation 5: A SUPPLEMENT TO A
HIGH SCHOOL DIPLOMA

The awarding of a diploma is evidence only that a student has (1) completed the required work in general education to the best of his ability, and (2) has finished satisfactorily a certain sequence of elective courses. In addition to the diploma, each student should be given a durable record of the courses studied in four years and the grades obtained. The existence of such a record should be well publicized so that employers ask for it rather than merely relying on a diploma when questioning an applicant for a job about his education. The record might be a card that could be carried in a wallet.

Recommendation 6: ENGLISH COMPOSITION

The time devoted to English composition during the four years should occupy about half the total time devoted to the study of English. Each student should be required to write an average of one theme a week.

Themes should be corrected by the teacher. In order that teachers of English have adequate time for handling these themes, no English teacher should be responsible for more than one hundred pupils.

To test the ability of each student in English composition, a schoolwide composition test should be given in every grade; in the ninth and eleventh grades, these composition tests should be graded not only by the teacher but by a committee of the entire school. Those students who do not obtain a grade on the eleventh-grade composition test commensurate with their ability as measured by an aptitude test should be required to take a special course in English composition in the twelfth grade.

In all the schools visited, at least three years of the study of English were required; in many schools, four. On the basis of conversations with teachers, I became convinced that half of this time should be devoted to English composition and that students, particularly those with academic ability, should be given ample opportunity through practice to develop their skill in English composition. English teachers were strongly of the opinion that, for the best instruction, themes should be corrected by the regular teacher, who, in turn, should discuss them with the students. Obviously, adequate instruction in English composition requires that teachers not be overloaded. In one school I visited, the use of composition tests as recommended above has been found a highly satisfactory device for improving the work in composition.

Recommendation 7: DIVERSIFIED PROGRAMS
FOR THE DEVELOPMENT
OF MARKETABLE SKILLS

Programs should be available for girls interested in developing skills in typing, stenography, the use of

clerical machines, home economics, or a specialized branch of home economics which through further work in college might lead to the profession of dietitian. Distributive education should be available if the retail shops in the community can be persuaded to provide suitable openings. If the community is rural, vocational agriculture should be included. For boys, depending on the community, trade and industrial programs should be available. Half a day is required in the eleventh and twelfth grades for this vocational work. In each specialized trade, there should be an advisory committee composed of representatives of management and labor. Federal money is available for these programs.

The school administration should constantly assess the employment situation in those trades included in the vocational programs. When opportunities for employment in a given trade no longer exist within the community, the training program in that field should be dropped. The administration should be ready to introduce new vocational programs as opportunities open in the community or area. In some communities, advanced programs of a technical nature should be developed; these programs often involve more mathematics than is usually required for the building trades or auto mechanics programs.

As stated in Recommendation 3 (a), p. 47, the students enrolled in programs which develop marketable skills should also be enrolled in English, social studies, and other courses required for graduation. Furthermore, efforts should be made to prevent isolation from the other students. Homerooms may be effective means to this end (see Recommendation 20, p. 74).

The reader of this report who is not familiar with educational terminology must keep in mind that the word *vocational* has a special connotation when used by high school people. A vocational program is usually one supported by federal money flowing through the state agency in charge of vocational education and matched by state funds. The conditions under which this money can be spent are generally defined by the Smith–Hughes and George–Barden Acts and specifically defined by the state supervising agency. As indicated earlier in this report, states vary greatly in the rules which they have adopted for the expenditure of these federal funds. The federally supported vocational programs must involve fifteen hours a week in the shops in the eleventh and twelfth grades and also require one period of related subjects such as mechanical drawing and mathematics. Examples of vocational subjects included are building trades, auto mechanics, the training of tool and die mechanics, printing, electrical work, metal trades including welding, and agriculture. In some schools essentially the same amount of time is devoted to the vocational work, although no federal funds are involved.

Excellent examples of vocational programs were found in a number of schools. To give one example, those boys enrolled in a building trades course built a house which was sold before the completion of their work. The money was put into a revolving fund for the building of a house by the succeeding class. I was assured in several communities that those who did well in the building trades program could find employment at once as carpenters. In other schools where no building trades program was in existence, the reason was the absence of employment opportunities for carpenters. I mention this particular situation as illustrating how necessary it is to tie vocational programs to employment opportunities in each community.

The training of tool and die mechanics requires expensive and elaborate machine shops. I was surprised how frequently I encountered such shops. I was impressed by the obvious interest of the students in shopwork. Programs for mechanics flourished in cities where the local trades were ready to employ those who had developed the skills requisite for a skilled workman fashioning tools and handling metals. I was told in several communities that the boys who had successfully completed such a program could at once obtain positions in local factories and gain a full year in an apprentice program. In some communities where there was a local junior college, high school graduates specializing in machine shop programs could study courses at the junior college level and, with the mastery of more applied mathematics, take the first step in becoming tool designers.

The line between the industrial arts program and the vocational shop program for boys is not an easy one to draw. One may say that the industrial arts program provides a survey of the different skilled trades involving the use of tools and the working of materials as diverse as leather, wood, and metal. In the schools in which there are strong vocational shop programs for boys, the industrial arts courses can be considered as preparatory or exploratory courses.

I observed that the presence of strong vocational work under the Smith–Hughes Act in a comprehensive high school provides somewhat the same stimulus to those in the industrial arts program as does the offering of a college-level course in the twelfth grade to all who have elected an academic program (p. 63). The fact that able boys are in a position to anticipate by at least a year the regular work of apprenticeship in the skilled trades means that the others who are doing shopwork see high standards of excellence before them. It seemed to me that the whole atmosphere in the industrial arts shops was more professional in those schools which had strong vocational programs than it was in the schools which did not.

Where local opportunities permit, students in some of the vocational programs may obtain experience by working on jobs outside the school. This work experience program has been expanded in recent years. Its success, I was told, depends on the close relationship between the supervisor of the schoolwork and the employer. The work on the job must be related to the work in the school. I found a few cases in which there was some dissatisfaction with this arrangement on the part of the school authorities because of the time the students were away from school. But more often the principal as well as the students regretted that there were not more opportunities available for providing students with work experience.

Distributive education in some localities has been developed to a high degree. In this program work experience is provided for both boys and girls in retail shops in the community. The program is usually elected more heavily by girls than by boys. Instruction in the school is related to the work on the job. Success depends on the number of openings in local stores and the attitude of the employer. I found only one school in which the principal had decided against this program and refused to introduce it.

For further details concerning vocational education the reader is referred to Appendix F (p. 123).

Recommendation 8: SPECIAL CONSIDERATION
FOR THE VERY SLOW READERS

Those in the ninth grade of the school who read at a level of the sixth grade or below should be given special consideration. These pupils should be instructed in English and the required social studies by special teachers who are interested in working with such students and who are sympathetic to their problems. Remedial reading should be part of the work, and special types of textbooks should be provided. The elective programs of these pupils should be directed toward simple vocational work, and they should be kept out of the regular vocational programs for boys, the distributive education program, and the regular commercial program for girls. These students should not be confused with mentally retarded students. The education of the mentally retarded is a special problem which in some states is also handled in the regular high school through special instruction and the use of special state funds.

In every school visited, a certain fraction of the entering class was composed of boys and girls whose reading ability was several grades below that of their classmates. For example, there might be as many as 10 or 15 per cent of the students reading at the fourth-, fifth-, or sixth-grade level. These slow readers have great difficulty with the required courses in English and social studies. Common practice was to include a few of these slow readers in each of the regular classes in English and social studies and to trust the skill of the teacher to develop these students' capacities through individual attention. Many teachers frankly admitted this task was an almost hopeless undertaking. If one book is used for the entire class, the slow readers are hardly able to read the book. In about half the schools I visited, some special provisions were made for this group of students. In only a few schools, however, were the provisions commensurate with the difficulties of the task. Nevertheless, there seems to be an increasing interest in this challenging educational problem.

The improvement of reading ability is, of course, the paramount problem, and work with remedial reading must be provided. However, in the opinion of teachers involved, it is very difficult, even with the best of instruction, to raise the reading level of these students more than two grades. Only a few are able to reach the degree of efficiency that enables them to enter regular classes in English and social studies later in their high school course. Whether or not greater attention to reading difficulties in the lower grades would have improved this situation in the schools I visited, I am not prepared to say. But those who are well informed about the teaching of reading emphasize that the development of reading skill must be a continuous process throughout the school years.

The whole problem of the instruction in the first eight grades and the relation of the inadequacies in this area to the problems of the high school is a subject on which I have no basis to report.

Recommendation 9: THE PROGRAMS OF THE
ACADEMICALLY TALENTED

A policy in regard to the elective programs of academically talented boys and girls should be adopted by the school to serve as a guide to the counselors. In the type of school I am discussing the following program should be strongly recommended as a minimum:

Four years of mathematics, four years of one foreign language, three years of science, in addition to the required four years of English and three years of social studies; a total of eighteen courses with homework to be taken in four years. This program will require at least fifteen hours of homework each week.

Many academically talented pupils may wish to study a second foreign language or an additional course in social studies. Since such students are capable of handling twenty or more courses with homework, these additional academic courses may be added to the recommended minimum program. If the school is organized on a seven- or eight-period day (Recommendation 12), at least one additional course without homework (for example, art or music) may also be scheduled each year.

If as school policy a minimum academic program including both mathematics and a foreign language is recommended to the academically talented pupils and their parents, the counselors will have the problem of identifying as early as possible the members of the group. It may well be that, in the next lower 10 or 20 per cent of the boys and girls in terms of scholastic aptitude on a national basis, there are

a number who ought to be guided into similar but less rigorous programs.

In some schools sequential courses in music theory and composition are offered which involve a considerable amount of homework. These are not the usual courses in music, however, which I encountered in my visits. Students with special aptitude for music might well be advised to elect such a sequence as an *addition* to the minimum program instead of a second foreign language. I do know, however, experienced public school administrators who would argue for the *substitution* of this sequence or a second language for twelfth-grade mathematics and twelfth-grade science in the case of girls. In this connection, I should like to point out that the above recommendation is in no way the equivalent of establishing a rigid academic track or labeled program. Since the recommendation is intended only as a guide to counselors, its adoption in no way prevents the counselor from advising exceptional programs in exceptional cases.

The essence of the recommendation is that students who have the ability to handle effectively both mathematics and a foreign language (by definition, the "academically talented," p. 20) should be urged to study both subjects in grades nine through twelve.

On a national basis, the group we are referring to as the "academically talented" constitutes about 15 per cent of the high school population. The percentage may be smaller or larger in particular schools, depending on the chance distribution of academic talent in a given year. National norms for aptitude tests will provide a rough guide as to what fraction of a given class in a school has academic ability corresponding approximately to that of the upper 15 per cent on a national basis. In giving advice to an individual student, the counselor should be guided by aptitude and achievement tests and by the success of the pupil each year as measured by his grades in the academic courses. In advising parents as to what courses are too difficult for their children, the counselor should likewise be guided by test data and by grades in courses. The recommended program is intended only for those students who have ability in *both* mathematics and foreign languages. If the counselor becomes convinced that a student is having difficulty with one or the other subject, he should then decide the student in question is not academically talented. For students of considerable academic ability in one field only, special programs should be devised. *If the scholastic aptitude test scores and lower grade records indicate that a student is in the upper 15 per cent on a national basis, the presumption should be that the recommended minimum academic program can be carried.*

In some schools, the main problem stems from the tendency of some academically talented pupils either to elect an easy program or to enroll in a vocational sequence to prepare for an immediate job. In other schools, the reverse situation is found: the main problem the counselor faces is persuading the overambitious parent of a child with little academic ability that eleventh- and twelfth-grade mathematics, physics, and foreign languages are too difficult.

The question might be raised as to why a school board should adopt the policy I have recommended. What are the arguments in favor of an academically talented student's electing a wide program of at least eighteen courses with homework? To my mind the most compelling argument is that the student in question has potentialities shared with only a relatively few contemporaries, probably not more than 15 per cent of his age group. If these potentialities are not developed as far as possible during the school years, they may never be fully developed. From the point of view of the individual, failure to develop talent in school may be the equivalent of locking many doors. For example, without mathematics and science in high school, it would be difficult later to enter an engineering school, to take a premedical course in college, and impossible to begin a scientific career in a university. If something approaching mastery of a foreign language is not attained before graduation from high school, it may never be attained.

The loss to the individual from not electing a suitable program in high school is clear. So too is the loss to the nation. From the 15 per cent of the youth who are academically talented will come the future professional men and women. These people ought to have as wide and solid an education as possible. It is in the national interest to have them develop their capacities to the full and to start this development as early as possible. My recommended program differs from many I have seen in that it is not a specialized program in either mathematics and science or in foreign languages. If a student completes this wide program in high school, his range of choice of college majors is far greater than if he had specialized earlier.

Concerning the Preparation for College   Some might argue for my recommendation by saying that the program outlined is the proper college-preparatory program. But those who argue this way lay themselves open to serious counterarguments. I have carefully avoided the use of the phrase "college-preparatory." To my mind, the academically talented youth ought to elect a full program of stiff courses in high school and ought to go to college. But the reasons for the first imperative are only distantly related to those that support the second. The fact of the matter is that today in the United States it is impossible to relate the details of a high school course of study to the subsequent work of a student in a college or university, unless the collegiate work is defined in very specific terms. Requirements for admission to an undergraduate engineering college can be clearly stated in terms of the knowledge of mathematics and science demanded in the freshman professional courses. But it would be out of the question for all colleges and universities to require a similar high school preparation in mathematics and science. There is such a wide variety of possible courses of study open to undergraduates in our colleges and universities that the concept of specific preparation for college work is almost without meaning. Even in institutions with a highly selective admission policy, it is possible for a very bright boy to complete with honors his college course although he enters with little knowledge of science, mathematics, or a foreign language. If he majors in history or English literature, for example, the only high school courses which can be regarded as direct preparation for college are those in

English and social studies. To be sure, such a young man will be forever handicapped by the fact that his potentialities were not fully developed in the high school years, but so far as his work in college is concerned, it could be maintained he had been "prepared."

Uniform standards for admission to college are impossible in the United States for a number of reasons. Even the degree of uniformity existing among the colleges that used the College Entrance Examination system of fifty years ago cannot be re-established. High school people naturally resist any attempt on the part of college admission officers to prescribe the content of courses or even the pattern of courses. And it must be remembered that from some communities many boys and girls of only average academic ability are propelled by social pressures toward a four-year college. For better or worse, in many sections of the country this type of student must be given at least an opportunity to try college work. In some states practically the only requirement for admission to the state-supported institutions of higher learning is the possession of a high school diploma. Private colleges exist that have no higher requirements for admission and in which those with little preparation and only a modicum of ability can obtain a bachelor's degree. In a word, the idea is completely illusory that the high school curriculum might be stiffened by agreement as to entrance requirements on the part of colleges and universities.

The Misinterpretation of the Results of Tests   The mounting numbers of potential college candidates have led to the requirements by an increasing number of collegiate institutions that candidates for admission take certain of the tests administered by the College Entrance Examination Board. These tests are quite different from the subject-matter examinations of even twenty-five years ago. Two types of objective test are used: one is aimed at measuring the student's aptitudes for scholastic work; the other, his achievement in certain subjects. These two types have been used in this study, as reported on page 33. Since there is considerable misunderstanding among citizens about the tests that are now given on a national scale, a few words on this subject may not be out of order. In the first place, one type of test (the SCAT, for example, page 33) is designed to measure aptitude. The distribution of the scores on such a test clearly does not indicate the quality of the teaching in a particular school. If one school has a mean score for the graduating class far higher than another, this differential does *not* mean that the first school is a better school than the other. If one thinks of these aptitude tests as measuring the brightness or dullness of the pupils, and the achievement tests as measuring how much pupils have learned, he is on fairly safe ground.

Scholarships are being awarded nationally on the basis of uniform tests. Since only the very top students in terms of aptitude can obtain high scores on these tests, a comparison of the success or failure of these pupils from different schools is in no way a valid comparison of the total education provided by the schools. To a large degree, it is a fortunate accident if a school has enrolled in its graduating class a few students with the very high aptitude necessary to do well in these tests. The school can indeed be proud if a student wins one of these awards, and the community should pay at least as much tribute to academic as to athletic talent. Obviously the school has directed the highly gifted student into a profitable course of study. No evidence is available from the outcomes of these national scholarship tests, however, as to what sort of program the majority of the academically talented elected, nor as to how successful, in general, are the teachers of the academic subjects.

Recommendation 10: HIGHLY GIFTED PUPILS

For the highly gifted pupils some type of special arrangement should be made. These pupils of high ability, who constitute on a national basis about 3 per cent of the student population, may well be too few in number in some schools to warrant giving them instruction in a special class. In this case, a special guidance officer should be assigned to the

group as a tutor and should keep in close touch with these students throughout their four years of senior high schoolwork. The tutor should see to it that these students are challenged not only by course work but by the development of their special interests as well. The identification of the highly gifted might well start in the seventh or eighth grade or earlier.

If enough students are available to provide a special class, these students should take in the twelfth grade one or more courses which are part of the Advanced Placement Program. This program has been developed in recent years by schools and colleges working cooperatively under the aegis of the College Entrance Examination Board. Under the program a student in the twelfth grade may take such courses as college mathematics, college English, or college history and, after passing suitable examinations, may be given college credit for the courses and also sophomore standing in these subjects. This program should be adopted not only because of the benefits which accrue to the students involved, but because it may well have a good influence on students of somewhat less ability by raising the tone of the whole academic program. Information about this program may be obtained by writing to the Director of the Advanced Placement Program, College Entrance Examination Board, 425 West 117th Street, New York 27, New York.

Recommendation 11: THE ACADEMIC INVENTORY

In order to provide meaningful statistics about the education of the academically talented, a school board through the superintendent should ask the principal each year to provide an academic inventory.

As explained earlier, the academic inventory summarizes the programs of the academically talented
students in the senior class without giving their
names. In a school in which the range of intellectual
ability corresponds to the national norm, 15 per cent
of the students would be included in this inventory.
In other schools the percentage may vary. The academic inventory should include information as to
what per cent of the academically talented boys and
girls went on to a two-year college, a four-year college, or a university. This academic inventory of the
graduating class might well be published each year.

It should be pointed out that, while the academic inventory is
at first sight a measure of the effectiveness of the counseling
service, such is often not the case. In the first place, the policy
of the school, as determined by the school board, superintendent, and principal, may slight foreign languages or may even
allow English and social studies to be neglected if the boys or
girls (usually the boys) are keen on taking the maximum
amount of mathematics and science. Furthermore, the elective
programs of the pupils always represent the resultant of the
counselors' advice and the pupils' and parents' interests and
desires. I might note here that the program I recommended
earlier for the academically talented is an elective program.
If it were required, there would be no need for an academic
inventory.

In Appendix H (p. 134) further details are given concerning the preparation of an academic inventory.

Recommendation 12: ORGANIZATION OF THE
SCHOOL DAY

The school day should be so organized that there are
at least six periods in addition to the required physical education and driver education which in many
states occupy at least a period each day. A seven- or

eight-period day may be organized with periods as short as forty-five minutes. Under such an organization, laboratory periods as well as industrial arts courses should involve double periods.

The flexibility provided by such an arrangement is to be contrasted with the rigidity of that of the six-period day. With a six-period day, one period of which is taken up by physical education, the academically talented student cannot elect the wide academic program recommended above and at the same time elect art, music, and practical courses. The importance of this recommendation can hardly be overemphasized in connection with the education of academically talented students.

Whether the school is organized into a six-, seven-, or eight-period day I found to be a matter of great importance as well as of controversy among school administrators. A number of administrators with whom I talked felt that a six-period day places the elective programs in a strait jacket. Therefore, these administrators have preferred a seven- or eight-period day with periods sometimes running as short as forty minutes. On the other hand, I met administrators who felt strongly that periods of nearly a full hour are essential and who urged that the school day be lengthened to make a seven-period day possible. In some places the school day is far too short.

Recommendation 13: PREREQUISITES FOR ADVANCED
ACADEMIC COURSES

Standards in advanced courses should be such that those who enroll in each successive course of a sequence have demonstrated the ability required to handle that course. To this end, admission to eleventh-grade mathematics should depend upon the student's receiving at least a *C* in tenth-grade mathematics, and for admission to twelfth-grade mathematics at least a *C* should be required in the eleventh-grade course. Similarly, if the physics course is given in the twelfth grade, it should be open only to those students who have studied three years of mathematics and obtained a grade of at least *C* in each course. Also, in the foreign language sequence, a grade of *C* should be required for entry into the second-year course.

Recommendation 14: STUDENTS SHOULD NOT BE GIVEN A RANK IN CLASS ACCORDING TO THEIR GRADES IN ALL SUBJECTS

In many schools, it is customary to designate a rank in class on graduation as determined by the marks received; the position of valedictorian is usually held by the student whose rank is number one. The ranking is calculated by averaging the grades in all subjects taken during the four years. I have found that in many schools the desire to rank high has led bright students to elect easy courses in order to obtain high grades. This fact emerges clearly from an examination of many programs sent to us by schools as part of their academic inventories. The use by some colleges and universities of rank in class as the basis of their admission policies has increased this tendency of bright boys and girls to avoid stiff programs. Following the practice in at least one school visited, I strongly recommend that the graduating class not be ranked on the basis of grades obtained in *all* subjects and that a valedictorian not be named on this basis. Admission officers in colleges and universities should be urged to examine the transcript of a student's entire record rather than to rely on the misleading rank in class.

Recommendation 15: ACADEMIC HONORS LIST

At the end of each marking period, a list should be published of the students who had elected courses recommended for the academically talented and had made an average grade of B. On graduation a notation might be made on the diploma if a student had placed on the academic honors list in all four years.

In order to provide an incentive for the election of a meaningful nonacademic sequence, those students whose achievement was outstanding in the courses that are usually labeled "commercial" or "vocational" should receive some special recognition. By such devices I believe the ambitions of students in various elective programs can be stimulated as much as by the granting of separate types of diploma.

Recommendation 16: DEVELOPMENTAL READING PROGRAM

A school should have the equipment for a developmental reading program. The program should be available on a voluntary basis for all the pupils in the school. The counselors and teachers of English should be asked to view this program sympathetically and to urge students to take advantage of the opportunity to increase reading speed and comprehension.

Developmental reading is not the remedial reading program designed for slow readers. Rather, it is a voluntary instructional program intended primarily to do three things: to help students acquire skill in different sorts of reading, from close and detailed reading to scanning; to increase reading speed; and to improve comprehension of the material read. Using equipment in a special room, students get a great deal of practice in reading and are able to test their speed. By appropriate tests, teachers check their comprehension.

Developmental reading programs have strong appeal for able students who understand the need for reading skills in subsequent college and university work. Teachers with whom I talked said that the ability of students in developmental reading classes had improved markedly. These teachers also insisted that enrollment in developmental reading should be on a voluntary basis since there seems to be a decided relationship between desire to improve and actual results.

Recommendation 17: SUMMER SCHOOL

The school board should operate a tuition-free summer school in which courses are available not only for students who have to repeat a subject, but also for the bright and ambitious students who wish to use the summer to broaden the scope of their elective programs.

Summer sessions for bright students have increased in number during recent years. The sessions are usually six weeks long and in a few instances have become very popular among the brighter students. The importance of this development for the academically talented student is obvious. It is possible for such a student to use the summer session to take either a practical course such as typing or an academic subject such as history. By the use of several summer sessions, a wider program can be elected than would otherwise be possible. Such is the case especially for students heavily engaged in extracurricular activities. The development of a summer session seems to me preferable to the lengthening of the school year.

Recommendation 18: FOREIGN LANGUAGES

The school board should be ready to offer a third and fourth year of a foreign language, no matter how few students enroll. The guidance officers should urge the completion of a four-year sequence of *one* foreign language if the student demonstrates ability in handling foreign languages. On the other hand, students who have real difficulty handling the first year of a language should be advised against continuing with the subject (Recommendation 13). The main purpose of studying a foreign language is to obtain something approaching a mastery of that language. And by a mastery is surely meant the ability to read the literature published in the language and, in the case of a modern language, to converse with considerable fluency and accuracy with an inhabitant of the country in question.

I have met no teachers of foreign language who felt that anything approaching mastery could be obtained by the study of a foreign language for only two years in high school, nor have the students felt that two years of study had given them any real working knowledge of the language. Four years of study, on the other hand, will yield dividends for those capable of handling foreign languages. This is the recommendation of the foreign language panel of the NEA Conference on the Identification and Education of the Academically Talented held in Washington in February, 1958.

Almost without exception, I found a deplorable state of affairs in regard to foreign languages. Too many students with limited ability were studying a foreign language for two years; too few able students were studying one language long enough. There appears to be a widespread feeling in the United States that there is considerable merit in a student's studying a language for two years—and only two years—in a high school.

Yet the foreign language teachers with whom I talked were almost unanimous in agreeing that two years were quite insufficient and that a very small residue, if any, was left in the student's mind after such an exposure. Even when a student's program included three or four years of a foreign language, it was very common to find that these three or four years were divided between the study of *two different* foreign languages.

Foreign language teachers complained of this situation, as did the bright students I interviewed when I met with the student leaders. Time and again I asked this question: "Why didn't you take three years of one language?" A frequent answer was: "Well, in their catalogues colleges only ask for two years." Or: "I wanted to take a third year, but there were only six or ten of us, and they will not give a third-year course unless there is a full class of at least twenty." I have found that students in general are interested in acquiring a real knowledge of a modern foreign language and in many cases have felt frustrated by the failure of school authorities to offer a third and fourth year. Occasionally, I found a third year offered, but the students were placed in the same classroom with the second-year students. The teacher always reported that such an arrangement was highly unsatisfactory.

It is hardly necessary to argue the importance of a foreign language in a world which has been so constricted by the invention of the airplane. Since, however, I have met some resistance among school people to my recommendation that all the academically talented youth should study four years of one foreign language, it may be well to remind the reader of the arguments in favor of this recommendation.

In the first place, unless a person has acquired something approaching mastery of one foreign language, he has missed an educational experience of the first importance. Such people never know what it means to *know* another language. They either think that acquiring mastery is an impossible hurdle to surmount, or else they believe that the ability to understand and speak a few words, perhaps enough to order a meal in a hotel, is a working knowledge. In short, a door is closed to them forever.

The second argument is the one usually put forward by foreign language teachers: that a real knowledge of a foreign language makes available a new approach to human problems. By reading the literature of another culture, one understands not only something of the culture, but realizes that ideas which English-speaking people accept as a matter of course may never have been formulated in a comparable way in another language and vice versa. It is particularly important for applied scientists to realize that, while mathematics is an international language, there are many words which are almost untranslatable from one language to another because the concepts they convey are somewhat alien. For example, I discovered in translating into German a book of mine on education with the aid of a bi-lingual collaborator that there is no German equivalent of "equality of opportunity."

The third and fourth arguments are practical ones and not unrelated to the highly constricted and deeply divided world in which we live. It is agreed by foreign language teachers that a person who has mastered one foreign language is in a position to learn a second with far greater ease than would otherwise be the case. This fact is true even if the second language is unrelated to the first. Therefore, a student who enters college with a considerable degree of mastery of one foreign language is able to pick up a second much more rapidly than he could otherwise. For example, one finds people in United States missions overseas who have the great-est difficulty learning the language of the country because they have never learned any foreign language.

Finally, it seems quite clear that a small fraction of our youth have those special talents which are needed for making rapid progress in the study of a foreign language. Unless such youth have an opportunity to find out that they are indeed highly gifted in this respect, their talents will never be developed. It is usually too late for such talents to be discovered and developed in the college years. Just as in the mathematics sequence in high school a few boys and girls are always discovered who are specially gifted in mathematics, so too if the foreign language sequence were as well developed as mathematics and science in our schools, those with equivalent linguistic talent would be discovered. One hardly need argue that such boys and girls will find fruitful and rewarding careers in the modern world. That the nation badly needs young people who can quickly master a foreign language for missions overseas, both official and private, is evident to all who read the daily news. The grim competition with the Soviet Union in newly developing countries turns quite as much on an adequate supply of competent linguists as on our ability to send competent engineers and businessmen to these nations.

One further word on the study of foreign languages. The movement is growing in the United States, sponsored by the leaders among the foreign language teachers, to start the instruction of the foreign languages in the lower grades. This instruction is to be given by teachers who speak the language in question fluently and with an acceptable accent. Speaking knowledge is developed before reading knowledge and without emphasis on grammar.

I do not venture to suggest the best method of teaching a foreign language. There is no doubt that very considerable progress has been made in developing new methods. Furthermore, there can be no question that children learn foreign languages more readily when they are young. Therefore, one can watch with interest the new developments which have started in a number of communities and which, it is hoped, will result in a considerable proportion of the eighth-grade students having a speaking knowledge and some degree of reading knowledge of a modern foreign language.

Thus far, I have seen only one school in which the transition from the lower grades to the high school level has been satisfactorily accomplished. That there are problems here, most of the experts in the field agree. And it is the final outcome with which a citizen must be concerned. In short, the question is whether a boy or girl ends his or her school years with something approaching a mastery of a foreign language.

It would be a great mistake if a school board put off making the necessary changes in the present high school offering with the excuse that foreign language instruction was to be developed in the grades. There is a time lag in education that must always be kept in mind. Development of foreign language instruction in the grades will not produce results for nine to fourteen years. This interval is too great. On the other hand, if a given high school adds a third and fourth year of a foreign language now, results will be evident in five or six years as college graduates take their place in national life as professional men and women.

Recommendation 19: SCIENCE COURSES

All students should obtain some understanding of the nature of science and the scientific approach by a required course in physical science or biology. This course should be given in at least three sections grouped by ability (Recommendation 4, p. 49).

To accommodate students who are interested in science but do not have the required mathematical ability, two types of chemistry courses should be offered. For entry into one, at least a C in algebra and tenth-grade mathematics should be required. The other course should be designed for pupils with less mathematical ability. The standards even in this second course, however, should be such that those with less than average ability (assuming a distribution of ability according to the national norm) will have difficulty passing the course.

In addition to the physics course given in the twelfth grade with mathematics as a prerequisite (Recommendation 13) another course in physics should be offered with some such designation as "practical physics." The standards in this second course should be such that students with less than average ability have difficulty passing the course.

Recommendation 20: HOMEROOMS

> For the purpose of developing an understanding between students of different levels of academic ability and vocational goals, homerooms should be organized in such a way as to make them significant social units in the school. To this end, students should be kept together in one homeroom for the entire senior high school course (three or four years), and care should be taken to have each homeroom a cross section of the school in terms of ability and vocational interest. The teachers in charge of the homerooms should be persuaded by the administration that their work as homeroom teachers is important. Sufficient time should be allotted to the homeroom so that students may use this period to develop a sense of community interest and to have practice in a small way in representative government. The homerooms should elect one or two representatives to the student council, and these representatives should report back after each meeting of the council. They should listen to the opinions of their constituents and be guided by their opinions in voting on matters before the student council. To be effective, the student council should be treated sympathetically by the school administrators so that there will be some important questions each year with which the student council can be concerned and which, in turn, can be presented to the homerooms by the representatives.

One of the highly important objectives of the comprehensive high school is the development of mutual respect and understanding between students with different abilities and different vocational interests. Indeed, in one school which I visited, the superintendent stated that one of his principal aims was to develop an attitude between the future manager of a factory and the future labor leader which would result in mutual respect and understanding. Such a strong democratic spirit, he said, was characteristic of his city. From my brief examination of the situation, I concluded he was right about the city and that his school was accomplishing the aim he had in mind.

Much as I believe in the importance of this aspect of public education, I should be quite unrealistic if I did not point out that in many communities there are blocks to the usefulness of the comprehensive high school as an instrument for developing a spirit of understanding between different groups. A school can make little progress against social pressures in a heavily polarized community.

Recommendation 21: TWELFTH-GRADE SOCIAL STUDIES

In the twelfth grade a course on American problems or American government should be required. This course should include as much material on economics as the students can effectively handle at this point in their development. Each class in this course should be a cross section of the school: the class should be heterogeneously grouped. Teachers should encourage all students to participate in discussions. This course should develop not only an understanding of the American form of government and of the economic basis of our free society, but also mutual respect and understanding between different types of students. Current topics should be included; free discussion of controversial issues should be encouraged. This approach is one significant way in which our schools distinguish themselves from those in totalitarian nations. This course, as well as well-organized homerooms and certain student activities, can contribute a

great deal to the development of future citizens of our democracy who will be intelligent voters, stand firm under trying national conditions, and not be beguiled by the oratory of those who appeal to special interests.

SECTION IV

High Schools with a Limited Degree of Comprehensiveness

A. The Small High School

The enrollment of many American public high schools is too small to allow a diversified curriculum except at exorbitant expense (p. 37). The prevalence of such high schools —those with graduating classes of less than one hundred students—constitutes one of the serious obstacles to good secondary education throughout most of the United States. I believe such schools are not in a position to provide a satisfactory education for any group of their students—the academically talented, the vocationally oriented, or the slow reader. The instructional program is neither sufficiently broad nor sufficiently challenging. A small high school cannot by its very nature offer a comprehensive curriculum. Furthermore, such a school uses uneconomically the time and efforts of administrators, teachers, and specialists, the shortage of whom is a serious national problem.

Financial considerations restrict the course offerings of the small high schools. As the curriculum is narrowed, so is the opportunity for a meaningful program. Unless a graduating class contains at least one hundred students, classes in advanced subjects and separate sections within all classes become impossible except with extravagantly high costs.

This statement I make on the basis of my own observations (schools *A* and *O*, Table 1, and a still smaller school which I visited for a day); the same conclusion has been reached by a committee of the American Association of School Administrators. The normal pattern of distribution of academic talent is such that a class of one hundred will have between fifteen and twenty academically talented students —those who can and should study effectively and rewardingly advanced courses in mathematics, science, and foreign languages as well as general education courses in English and social studies. A slightly smaller number of less bright students will, if they work hard, be able to study a somewhat less intensive program. In a class of one hundred, these two groups together will barely provide sufficient enrollment to justify the school's offering advanced academic courses. If the graduating class were much smaller, these two groups together would be too small to warrant a properly organized sequential program in mathematics, science, and foreign languages. The reluctance of academically talented girls to study advanced science and mathematics courses exists also in small high schools and adds to the financial difficulty of offering such courses.

A common practice in small high schools in an effort to deal with these problems is to require all students, regardless of ability or interest, to take an academic program. The nonacademically talented student is seldom able to follow vocational goals and to develop general interests. Although he constitutes a majority of the student body, he is obliged to study courses which at best only the top quarter of his class can pursue with profit. With a small enrollment grouping by ability is difficult, and this student often becomes bored and frustrated. Furthermore, his presence in these courses tends to affect adversely the tone of instruction and to encourage a lowering of grading standards.

In many of the really small high schools there are only

a few teachers. The scope even of the academic program is correspondingly limited. Courses are often not offered in advanced mathematics, physics or chemistry, and foreign languages, or are offered only every other year. Where there are such courses, they are often taught by teachers whose training in the subject-matter area is inadequate and insufficient. Personnel services such as guidance also tend to be nonexistent or to become the additional responsibilities of the administrator or teachers who lack professional training in these fields. To the extent that there are trained specialists, there is waste. There are not enough students to warrant the full-time services of such specialists.

The same waste occurs in the case of teachers in some fields. A properly qualified physics or mathematics teacher has only limited opportunities in a small high school. He is obliged to teach such subjects as general science and biology on the one hand, or general mathematics and business arithmetic on the other, in addition to his field of special competence. Thus a very scarce national asset is squandered.

Elimination of the small high school on a nationwide basis will help reduce the teacher shortage in important subject-matter areas. For example, in 1956 approximately twelve thousand of the nation's twenty-one thousand public high schools with senior classes offered at least one course in physics. (The total number of high schools was about twenty-five thousand, but of those some four thousand were junior high schools which did not offer physics.) There must have been at least twelve thousand physics teachers. If there is to be no reduction in the number of high schools, at least another nine thousand teachers qualified to teach physics are required to insure all of our academically talented youth an opportunity to study this important subject. To the degree that some of the twelve thousand teachers are not well qualified, even more will be required. On the other hand, if the number of high schools could be reduced to something like nine thousand which, as will be explained below, are enough to educate American youth today if the schools are of sufficient size (with a graduating class of at least one hundred), there would no longer be a shortage of teachers in this highly important field. The chances would be good that all students who can profit from studying physics would be able to get adequate instruction.[1]

Appendix G (p. 132) shows the seriousness of the small high school problem in the entire country. Even in New Jersey, the state with the fewest small high schools, 16 per cent of the high schools are of inadequate size. Throughout the whole country, more than 70 per cent of the high schools are in this category.

An analysis of the percentage of the seniors attending small high schools presents a less dismal, but still not satisfactory, picture, except perhaps in California and New Jersey, where less than 10 per cent of the seniors attend high schools which are too small. In California the small high school problem has been almost eliminated; 95 per cent of the youth enrolled in public high schools are attending schools with a graduating class of one hundred or more. Across the nation, just over 30 per cent of twelfth-grade students attend high schools which are too small to do an adequate job. In other words, one out of every three seniors attends a school in which the chances are slim that he can get a satisfactory secondary education.

How Many High Schools Should There Be?   There are approximately four thousand high schools[2] with graduating

---

[1] The statistics in this section are based on the figures contained in a pamphlet, "Offerings and Enrollments in Science and Mathematics in Public High Schools 1956," published by the U.S. Office of Education.

[2] According to our data in Appendix G, there are 18,527 schools, of which 14,184 are too small (excluding Georgia, for which information was not available). According to the U.S. Office of Education, the latest total figure is 21,000.

classes of at least one hundred and some seventeen thousand high schools with graduating classes of less than one hundred. There are approximately a million and a half twelfth-grade students in the United States. Approximately one million of them attend the four thousand high schools of sufficient size. If the remaining five hundred thousand now scattered among the other 17,000 high schools were distributed uniformly in high schools with graduating classes of one hundred, five thousand high schools would be needed. The total number of high schools would then be nine thousand (the present four thousand of sufficient size plus the additional five thousand). Since some of these new high schools might well have graduating classes larger than one hundred, it is safe to assume that nine thousand is the *maximum* number of high schools needed in the United States at this time. It is worth noting that California accommodates one hundred forty thousand seniors in 481 high schools and that if all the other states did as well proportionately, the million and a half seniors in the United States could be handled in just over five thousand high schools!

These estimates are based on current data. A few years from now, when the vast increase in the size of the age group will be reflected in the increased number of high school seniors, these estimates will need revision. Some high schools now too small will become large enough; but it is highly unlikely the percentage of youth attending small high schools will drastically diminish.

If the total number of high schools on a nationwide basis were reduced from about twenty-one thousand to approximately nine thousand, secondary instruction throughout the land would thereby be generally improved. Teachers and other professional personnel would be made available, and their talents could be used more effectively. Almost all academically talented youth would be able to study physics, for example, not only without there being any increased need for teachers, but also under an arrangement that would have virtually eliminated the so-called "teacher shortage" in this field.

Another important result of the reduction in the number of small high schools would be an increase in opportunities for citizen action to improve schools. The number of high schools in which each state citizens committee might be interested would become manageable. Committees would be able to promote such statewide projects as an academic inventory without putting an undue strain on their resources. Only in New York and Texas would state committees have to deal with more than six hundred high schools (see Appendix G); and, since eighty-seven of New York's schools would be in New York City and would constitute a unique problem by themselves, only the Texas committee would face a really serious problem of numbers.

How Can Small High Schools Be Eliminated?   Experience in those states that have been most successful in eliminating the small high school through district reorganization shows that imaginative leadership is necessary at the state level in order to promote the necessary local action.

The state department of education must initiate planning for school district reorganization on a statewide basis. A carefully prepared plan, like New York's Master Plan, is a necessary first step. It shows what has to be done to insure high schools of sufficient size through reorganization. The Master Plan does not have legislative force but merely serves as a guide. However, the New York state legislature has taken several steps to encourage local initiative and generally to facilitate the accomplishment of the Plan's objectives. The chief state school officer has the power to initiate specific reorganization proposals. He can propose the creation of a new school district. The people make the ultimate decision but vote on a districtwide basis throughout the proposed district. Thus, unlike the situation in states where the electorate votes on a district-by-district basis in each of the old districts, very narrow interests are not likely to have an overriding influence on the results. For example, residents in the parts of the proposed district with a larger property valuation behind each student are inclined to be unenthusiastic about supporting the education of the children of their less fortunate neighbors. When each of the districts to be included in a new district has to vote approval on an individual basis, as, for example, in Iowa and Indiana, the wealthier areas tend to block reorganization.

New York has also shown that a state legislature must offer financial inducements to encourage local enlightenment. The state offers reorganized districts special assistance for transportation and building costs, two items that press most heavily on a newly enlarged district. The state also offers additional aid for operating costs on a sliding scale, in which the additional amount is proportionately greater in the smaller reorganized districts but decreases gradually as districts increase in size.

Without a carefully considered plan, reorganization will probably lead to the elimination of many one-room common schools and not produce many new high schools whose graduating classes have at least one hundred students. The statistics of what has been accomplished in the way of reducing the number of school districts then look good, but the small high schools are not necessarily affected by the reorganization.

Undoubtedly there are certain parts of the United States where geographic considerations make small high schools necessary. Population is so sparsely distributed that enough pupils just cannot be effectively transported to a central point. However, successful experience in certain parts of the wide-open spaces of Texas and the remote forest country of the Far West shows that much more can be done elsewhere to eliminate the small high school than is being done at present. I visited a school which was drawing pupils from approximately three thousand square miles; many of the children had a bus ride of an hour and a half each way. A balance must be struck between the benefits derived from education in a high school of sufficient size and the deleterious effects of a long bus ride to and from school each day. Geography may sometimes be legitimate justification for a small high school, but all too often it is merely an excuse. Human nature—not geography—offers the real explanation.

Imaginative leadership, shrewd political thinking, and a willingness to offer "an alluring carrot" have been effective in promoting school district reorganization in New York, California, and a few other states. For example, in New York, in addition to the incentives noted above, the state education department provides professional leadership to districts wishing to study reorganization. The department gives superintendents, principals, boards of education, and citizens groups an opportunity to meet around a conference table with experts in secondary education to study how reorganization will bring specific improvements in the secondary school program. Specialists in school transportation and school buildings discuss needs in these areas. Finally, the department's school finance specialists work out the costs of operating the reorganized district, the State aid, and the approximate tax rates. Having secured this information, local districts are then prepared to vote with understanding on proposals for school district reorganization.

In other states, less informed interests dominate. High schools remain small. These states just cannot make their proper contributions to the national effort. If citizens in these states face up to the implications of their failure to act, action may be forthcoming.

B. *The Large City High School*

Public education in the large cities presents certain problems which are not to be found in smaller communities; furthermore, in the older cities, tradition often plays a determining role. It is usual for large urban high schools to provide instruction for all the youth of a given district in the city, with the exception of those boys interested in vocational programs. In most of the large cities in the East and Middle West, there are one or more vocational high schools to which boys may go, regardless of the district in which they live. The existence of these vocational schools means that the facilities for shopwork in the general high schools of the city are limited, and the work provided in the shops is essentially of an industrial arts nature. The commercial program for girls, however, may be offered in these general high schools in the different sections of a city to the same degree as in other communities—that is, to the degree that the families involved are interested in having their children elect this type of program.

Because of the size and complexity of the school system in a large city, the superintendent's office has a number of responsibilities not to be found in the corresponding offices in cities or communities where there are not more than two or three high schools. The centralized superintendent's office is able to provide special services, including research, for all the schools in the city. This service applies particularly to a testing program. For example, special projects for the identification and education of academically talented youngsters from culturally poor backgrounds are being developed. There are usually many such children in a large city, and the centralized school office has the facilities to implement these projects.

In most of the large cities, one finds a variety of districts, differing because of the type of families resident in them. I have been in large cities where some high schools are serving a district which is essentially composed of the families of professional men with college degrees; in such a district the parental desires orient the great majority of the students toward a four-year college or university. The problems faced by the principal and the counselors are essentially those which are to be found in certain types of suburban schools. These problems are considered in the section which follows. In other districts the proportion of the children who wish to go on to college may be less than 10 per cent of the graduating class. Such a district may be served primarily by a vocational high school which includes in its offerings an academic program with special emphasis on mathematics and science.

The relation of the vocational schools to the other high schools varies from city to city. For example, one of my staff visited an eastern city with a population of over one-half million which has a very heavy concentration of industry. There are strong vocational programs at the secondary school level: seven of the fourteen high schools are vocational or technical. One-half of the boys attend these schools, admission to which is on a selective basis. Vocational education enjoys the respect of the community. I know of no other city in which the academic rather than the vocational schools complain about being dumping grounds and in which there is not a stigma attached to being a vocational student.

It would be a task in itself to report on the high school situation in any one of the major cities of the United States. In some of them, something approaching a sociological revolution is in progress because of the rapid change in the backgrounds of the families resident in the city. For reasons explained earlier in this report, I have made no attempt to make even a preliminary study of the special problems of the high schools in the large cities. I have, however, visited the superintendents of several of these cities and, therefore, know something of the over-all situation. In addition, some of my staff have spent time in various types of schools in the large cities both along the East Coast and in the Midwest.

As to the education of vocational students in separate schools, one can only say that from the point of view of economy this arrangement seems to be the only practical scheme in many of these cities. The school boards are unwilling, as a rule, to allocate sufficient money to each of the high schools in a large city to purchase equipment necessary for a full vocational program. Furthermore, since the employment unit is the city itself, it would be difficult for vocational programs for boys in a comprehensive high school in a single district to reflect the over-all employment situation. It is almost impossible to have effective labor and management advisory committees at the district level. On the other hand, such committees can function satisfactorily at a citywide level in advising a centralized vocational high school or two or three such high schools. All these considerations merely illustrate once again the fact that in discussing vocational programs one has to take into account the nature of the community the high school serves and the employment situation.

In many of the eastern cities of considerable size and in a few of the medium-sized cities, one finds specialized high schools for the academically talented youth and for those with other talents. For example, in New York City the following specialized high schools have been developed over the years:

High School of Commerce
High School of the Performing Arts
High School of Music and Art
Food Trades Vocational High School
High School of Fashion Industries
Manhattan High School of Aviation Trades
New York School of Printing
Bronx High School of Science
Brooklyn High School of Automotive Trades
Brooklyn High School for Homemaking
    and twenty-three other specialized schools.

The argument in favor of the specialized high school for those with artistic or dramatic talent is similar to the argument for specialized vocational programs in one or more high schools in a large city—the presence of a large number of youth with special talents. There would not be enough students involved in such programs in smaller communities to warrant the establishment of this type of high school.

High schools which are reserved for the education of those of considerable academic ability have existed for many years in the large eastern cities. It is an interesting historic fact that although these selective academic high schools have flourished along the East Coast, they never seemed to have spread into the Middle or Far West. There is an interesting correlation, probably not accidental, between the absence of a large and powerful state university and the presence of selective academic high schools in the large cities of a given state.

I think no one familiar with the work of these selective academic high schools would challenge the fact that they are functioning in a very satisfactory manner and that they are providing a good academic education for the academically talented students who enroll in them. A characteristic of these schools is the ability of the administration to select those students who are admitted. The selection may be made on the basis of written examinations or on the basis of scores made on the type of test usually called a scholastic aptitude or intelligence test. In some of these schools, those who have less academic ability than the top 25 per cent are excluded on the basis of these tests. In their selective features these schools are reminiscent of the pre-university school in Europe which prepares students for examination for the state certificate required for admission to all the state universities. They differ from the preuniversity European schools in two respects: *first*, the course is shorter—the six-year Boston Latin School comes nearest the European school in regard to the length of the course; *second*, the failures are comparatively few—that is to say, for the most part, American selective academic high schools do not force any considerable percentage of their students to leave school because of failure to meet the required standards. On the other hand, I have visited preuniversity schools in Switzerland where only a third of those who enrolled completed satisfactorily the eight-year course, and many had dropped out at the halfway point.

From a social point of view, some of the advantages which accrue to pupils in the type of high school I have visited and about which I have reported in Section II, are not available to the students in the selective academic high school. The student body in this type of school is essentially homogeneous from the point of view of ability and vocational goals: all are headed for college and university work, and many intend to become professional men and women. It is only fair to point out that in the high school whose comprehensiveness is considerably limited by the nature of the community (page 13), the student also has little if any occasion to meet students with a different vocational interest, though he is certain to meet some with a considerably different degree of academic ability.

So far as I can ascertain, there is only one city in which a selective academic high school now enrolls a large fraction of the academically talented boys and girls of the city in question. Except in Boston, there seem to be always in existence in the same city several high schools of a somewhat comprehensive nature which also enroll a considerable number of academically talented youth and which are believed to give as satisfactory an academic education to the more able as do the selective high schools. Certainly these comprehensive high schools provide a recognized road to a college or university. This being the case, there has not been in the United States in recent years the real equivalent of a European preuniversity school, which provides the *only* secondary course for the academically talented and is the *only* type of school from which one may go to a university.

It is sometimes forgotten that the size of the city, the diversity of its inhabitants, and the existence of many other high schools reduce undue pressures on the school boards for admission of unqualified students to the selective academic high school. If such a school were set up in a smaller city and became recognized as the only good school for those who wished to go to college, parental pressure would become considerable. One doubts that a selective admission policy could be maintained for the same reasons that many selective academic high schools have not been able to follow the example of the European preuniversity schools and eliminate a fraction of each class by failure each year.

I should not want to argue for the elimination of selective academic high schools in the cities in which these schools are now successful, but I would raise many questions about the establishment of such a school in another city of equal size and more serious questions still if such a school were to be suggested for a city served by only a few high schools. The historical traditions of the selective schools in the East are well-known factors in their success. Furthermore, if my conclusions in Section II are correct, it is unnecessary to establish selective academic high schools for the education of the academically talented. As I have pointed out earlier in this report, with relatively minor changes many comprehensive high schools could provide a highly satisfactory education for this group. The improvement of the comprehensive high school would seem to offer far more promise for the improvement of American education than the introduction of selective academic high schools into communities where, hitherto, they have not existed.

C. *The Suburban High School**

High schools in areas that are adjacent to metropolitan cities and tributary to them are usually known as "suburban" high schools. They are commonly of three types, depending upon the nature of the areas they serve. Some of them are as widely comprehensive as are schools in independent cities, with subjects covering the whole range of offerings. Others have few if any students in the college-preparatory group and see their major task as that of helping their students develop marketable skills by graduation time. A rather sizable number emphasize heavily the college-preparatory function, often to the exclusion of any truly vocational program of the Smith-Hughes sort.

It is this third type that is commonly thought of as *the* suburban high school. But it is useful to give this phrase a wider meaning, since there are high schools which, because of the socioeconomic nature of the communities they serve, send a large majority of their graduates on to college, al-

* This section of the report is based largely on the experience and observations of Messrs. Youngert, Miller, and Ober.

though these schools are not located in what is strictly a suburb. In this report, for the purposes of clarity, I refer to schools in which a large majority of the students have collegiate ambitions as suburban high schools, wherever they may be located. A number of such schools have acquired excellent reputations throughout our country, largely because they are well financed and have been able to build strong administrative, guidance, and teaching staffs. The parents are very ambitious for their children, often to the point of wanting them prepared not only for college, but for specific colleges. In fact, parental ambitions in many cases outrun student abilities. In these schools, it is not unusual for the college-preparatory group to be 75 per cent or more of the student body and for the academic influence to go even beyond that figure and put a stigma on "practical" courses that help students get jobs immediately upon graduation.

The student body in the suburban high schools (as I am using the term) is often markedly higher in academic ability as measured by scholastic aptitude tests than the student bodies in other types of high school. At the same time, among the students are some of quite low mental ability and others who are weak in reading and in motivation. However, motivation is generally high, and is getting higher as the fear grows that college admission will be harder to achieve in the years that lie ahead.

One charge against suburban high schools has been that their courses of study meet the needs of their academic students well but not the needs of the relatively few who are not academic, some of whom may well be so slow in reading as to be unsuited to the regular run of classes. This charge applies only to some suburban high schools. Others are leading the way in adapting their curricula to their students and in devising desirable innovations. For instance, these schools have been pioneers in the development of good guidance programs, both because of their ability to afford them and because of the increasing need for guidance programs.

The main concern of the counselor in a suburban high school is often with the overambitious parent who wants his offspring to go to a particular college, even if the pupil has less-than-average academic ability. Such parents must be made to realize as soon as possible the limits nature has placed upon their ambitions; early individualized attention is required. Insistent pressure from parents on behalf of their children does make professional work on the part of the staff difficult, but at the same time it may serve as a driving force toward improvement of the school. Parents demand results and reject excuses, and sensible schools devise means to satisfy the demands, so long as they are constructive or can be made so. For example, the often excessive pressure for academic enrollment for children of widely varying abilities results in the grouping of students by ability in both the required subjects and the academic elective program. Without such grouping, the quality of instruction is impaired. Bright students become disinterested and bored, and average students become confused and frustrated.

While these pressures do have constructive results, they can have deleterious results also. The answer to this latter situation is *policy*—defensible policy. For instance, the guidance department must have it as policy that parents who want their children prepared for colleges for which they obviously are unsuited will be resisted. Such a policy does not mean that students will be barred from attempting preparation for those colleges, but it does mean that it is the duty of the counselors to do all they can to defend students against the unreasonable academic demands of their parents. It takes courage, but if counselors are professionally competent and agree as to policy they can act together in the best interests of the students. This same principle applies to other unreasonable parental pressures that may arise, among which a common one is the request that students be allowed to be absent from school for a longer period than the regular holiday in order that the family may have a more extended vacation period. A policy on such a subject, even a hard-boiled one, will gain acceptance—perhaps a grudging acceptance—if it is adhered to. Submission to unreasonable pressures weakens the school and increases the pressures until finally the teaching program itself suffers decline. The protection of the school lies in *policy*.

In a suburban high school, as already noted, almost all parents desire to have their children go to college. The inability of some of these children to do well in advanced academic areas points to the need for a sound array of non-academic electives; such as music, art, commercial subjects, industrial arts, and home economics. As a rule, these subjects are well taught and are included in the electives that some colleges will accept for entrance into the freshman class. They also prepare students for immediate employment.

Another innovation in which some of the suburban high schools have played a leading role is the Advanced Placement Program. That suburban high schools should have had a large part in the initiation of the program (see p. 63) can be understood by those who have known not only the pressure of parents for good high school education for their children but the desire, also, of able youth for challenging work.

There are some suburban high schools serving communities in which the collegiate ambitions of the parents, although great, are not too specific and can therefore be satisfied by the admission of their children to any one of a great variety of colleges. The social mores may be such that only a very few of the bright students are willing to enroll in tough academic programs which demand fifteen to twenty hours of homework each week. It is an uneven contest when the choice between easy and tough programs is left to students with convertibles, plenty of money, and community approval for spending most of their evenings in social activities. Obviously, in such cases the counselors and faculty face special problems. One problem is urging the academically talented students to work up to their capacity rather than merely meeting the minimum requirements of admission to those colleges where little more than a high school diploma is needed.

In all suburban high schools one of the main tasks of the guidance officer is college placement. These high schools send their graduates to a tremendous variety of institutions of higher learning located in all parts of our country. To keep the lines of communication open with these institutions and to follow high school graduates in their college careers require the services of one person working full time on college placement.

Although, because of the nature of their communities and student bodies, these suburban high schools *are* different, they still are like other high schools in that they can be judged by most of the criteria that have been used in this study for the evaluation of widely comprehensive high schools.

A Concluding Word

More than once in the course of this report, I have pointed to the diversities among our tax-supported schools. I have reported not only on the diversity of solutions of pedagogic problems but also on the diversity of the communities served by the high schools I have visited. I cannot emphasize too strongly the differences I have found between small industrial cities, suburban areas, and the districts I have visited in certain large cities. I hope this last section of the report has conveyed to the reader some idea of the way the problems faced by school administrators often depend on the attitudes of the families in the city or town in question. If I have made myself clear, it will be evident that there is no such thing as a typical American high school. Furthermore, it is impossible to draw a blueprint of an ideal high school. A school that would be highly satisfactory in a small industrial city would be unsatisfactory in many suburban areas, and vice versa. Within a large city great diversity will be found from district to district; it would be most unwise to attempt to say what is the correct curriculum or organization of all the high schools under the management of the city school board.

As I have already stated, I am convinced American secondary education can be made satisfactory without any radical changes in the basic pattern. This can only be done, however, if the citizens in many localities display sufficient interest in their schools and are willing to support them. The improvements must come school by school and be made with due regard for the nature of the community. Therefore, I conclude by addressing this final word to citizens who are concerned with public education: avoid generalizations, recognize the necessity of diversity, get the facts about your local situation, elect a good school board, and support the efforts of the board to improve the schools.

APPENDIXES

Appendix A: STATES INCLUDED IN STUDY

California
Colorado
Connecticut
Delaware
Illinois
Indiana
Iowa
Kansas
Kentucky
Maryland
Massachusetts
Michigan
Minnesota

Missouri
New Jersey
New York
Ohio
Oregon
Pennsylvania
Rhode Island
Texas
Utah
Vermont
Virginia
Washington
Wisconsin

Appendix B: SCHOOLS VISITED

* 1. A. C. Davis High School, Yakima, Washington
* 2. Alexander Ramsey Senior High School, St. Paul, Minnesota
* 3. Allentown High School, Allentown, Pennsylvania
* 4. Ann Arbor High School, Ann Arbor, Michigan
  5. Argenta High School, Argenta, Illinois
  6. Arsenal Technical High School, Indianapolis, Indiana
* 7. Austin High School, Austin, Minnesota
* 8. Bakersfield High School, Bakersfield, California
* 9. Barberton High School, Barberton, Ohio
* 10. Bedford High School, Bedford, Ohio
  11. Bloomfield High School, Bloomfield, New Jersey
* 12. Bloomington High School, Bloomington, Indiana
* 13. Broad Ripple High School, Indianapolis, Indiana
  14. Bronx High School of Science, New York
* 15. Carthage High School, Carthage, Texas
* 16. Central High School, Kalamazoo, Michigan
* 17. Central High School, Philadelphia, Pennsylvania
* 18. Central High School, Sheboygan, Wisconsin
* 19. Central School District No. 1, Suffern, New York
* 20. Chadsey High School, Detroit, Michigan
  21. Chadwicks High School, Chadwicks, New York
  22. DeAnza High School, El Sobrante (Richmond), California
  23. East Grand Rapids High School, East Grand Rapids, Michigan
  24. East High School, Denver, Colorado
  25. East High School, Salt Lake City, Utah
  26. Eastern High School, Lansing, Michigan
* 27. Edsel Ford High School, Dearborn, Michigan
* 28. Elkhart High School, Elkhart, Indiana
  29. Elyria High School, Elyria, Ohio
* 30. Franklin High School, Portland, Oregon
  31. George Washington High School, San Francisco, California
* 32. Gladewater Junior–Senior High School, Gladewater, Texas
* 33. Gloucester High School, Gloucester, Massachusetts

34. H. Fletcher Brown Vocational School, Wilmington, Delaware
* 35. Hibbing High School, Hibbing, Minnesota
* 36. Jackson High School, Jackson, Michigan
* 37. John Marshall High School, Richmond, Virginia
38. J. Sterling Morton High School, Cicero, Illinois
39. J. W. Sexton High School, Lansing, Michigan
40. Kingston High School, Kingston, New York
41. Lakeview Junior-Senior High School, Lakeview, Illinois
42. Leonia High School, Leonia, New Jersey
* 43. Lincoln Junior High School, Minneapolis, Minnesota
* 44. Lincoln High School, Manitowoc, Wisconsin
45. Macon High School, Macon, Illinois
* 46. Mansfield Senior High School, Mansfield, Ohio
47. Manteca Union High School, Manteca, California
* 48. Manual High School, Peoria, Illinois
49. Manual Training High School, Denver, Colorado
50. Maroa High School, Maroa, Illinois
51. Moline Senior High School, Moline, Illinois
* 52. Mont Pleasant High School, Schenectady, New York
53. Mount Diablo High School, Concord, California
54. Mount Zion High School, Mount Zion, Illinois
55. Myrtle E. Miller School of Special Education, St. Joseph, Missouri
56. Napa Union High School, Napa, California
* 57. New Albany High School, New Albany, Indiana
58. New Hartford High School, New Hartford, New York
* 59. Newton High School, Newtonville, Massachusetts
60. New York Mills High School, New York Mills, New York
61. Niantic High School, Niantic, Illinois
* 62. North Bennington High School, North Bennington, Vermont
* 63. North High School, Hagerstown, Maryland
* 64. North High School, Sheboygan, Wisconsin
* 65. N. R. Crozier Technical High School, Dallas, Texas
66. Oak Park and River Forest High School, Oak Park, Illinois

    67. Oriskany High School, Oriskany, New York
    68. Palo Alto Senior High School, Palo Alto, California
* 69. Peoria High School, Peoria, Illinois
* 70. Plainfield High School, Plainfield, New Jersey
* 71. Princeton High School, Princeton, New Jersey
    72. Proviso Township High School, Maywood, Illinois
* 73. Quincy Senior High School, Quincy, Illinois
* 74. Richmond Senior High School, Richmond, Indiana
    75. Rock Island High School, Rock Island, Illinois
* 76. San Bernardino High School, San Bernardino, California
    77. San Raphael High School, San Raphael, California
* 78. Santa Rosa High School, Santa Rosa, California
    79. Saydel High School, Des Moines, Iowa
* 80. Sewanhaka High School, Floral Park, New York
* 81. Shawnee High School, Louisville, Kentucky
* 82. Shortridge High School, Indianapolis, Indiana
    83. Sir Francis Drake High School, San Anselmo, California
* 84. Sommerville High School, Sommerville, New Jersey
    85. Southern Regional High School, Ocean County, New Jersey
* 86. South Fork High School, Miranda, California
* 87. South High School, Hagerstown, Maryland
    88. South High School, Salt Lake City, Utah
* 89. South Oak Cliff High School, Dallas, Texas
    90. Springfield Senior High School, Springfield, Ohio
* 91. Stephen Austin High School, Houston, Texas
    92. Stephen F. Decatur Senior High School, Decatur, Illinois
    93. Thomas Downey High School, Modesto, California
    94. Tracy Joint Union High School, Tracy, California
* 95. Tyler High School, Tyler, Texas
    96. Warrensburg Latham High School, Warrensburg, Illinois
* 97. Washington Park High School, Racine, Wisconsin
    98. West High School, Salt Lake City, Utah
    99. Whitesboro High School, Whitesboro, New York
* 100. William Horlick High School, Racine, Wisconsin

101. Wilmington High School, Wilmington, Delaware
* 102. Woodruff High School, Peoria, Illinois
* 103. York Community High School, Elmhurst, Illinois

School Systems Visited

* 1. Baltimore School System, Baltimore, Maryland
2. Buffalo School System, Buffalo, New York
* 3. Chicago School System, Chicago, Illinois
* 4. Cleveland School System, Cleveland, Ohio

* A school Dr. Conant visited personally.

Appendix C: CRITERIA FOR EVALUATING A COMPREHENSIVE HIGH SCHOOL

Table 1 on page 24 summarizes my judgment on a number of points which I investigated in the schools I visited. The last group of items in the table are taken from the academic inventory which was provided by the school after the visit. The results of the academic inventory are given in more detail in Appendix D.

The first three items (adequate instruction in English composition and social studies and ability grouping in required subjects) concern what I call the program in general education. The judgments of the first two items, recorded by the presence or absence of the plus signs for each school, are highly subjective. They are based on our conversations with the teachers, the students, and, in many cases, a visit to one or more classes. Since in every case two of us visited the school in question and our judgments usually coincided, they are not purely individual opinions. However, it might well be that if I had stayed in the school in question a week instead of a day my judgment of the adequacies or inadequacies of instruction in English composition and social studies would have changed. Therefore, these first two items in the table are to be viewed only as an indication of my impressions. But they do emphasize my belief in the importance of the instruction in these two areas. In addition to the adequacies in instruction in English composition, one should, of course, consider the adequacies of instruction in English and American literature. This instruction would be much harder to assess even if a visitor were to spend several days in the school and concern himself only with this subject.

The judgment expressed on Item 1 is compounded of two factors. First was the work load of the individual English teacher. I did not consider instruction in English composition satisfactory where I found a single teacher responsible for as many as 180 pupils. Second was the attitude of the English teachers toward the importance of English composition. It is worth noting that in a number of schools the students themselves felt that they should have been required to write more themes.

With regard to the judgment expressed in Item 2, it is my

opinion, again based on talking to teachers, that at least three years of social studies are an essential part of the general education program. In all the schools in which I judged the instruction in social studies to be adequate, with possibly one or two exceptions, at least three years were required of all. In every case, this requirement included one year of the study of American history and often one year of world history. The instruction in American history, judged by my conversations with the teachers, visits to classes, and discussions with the students, seemed to me in many cases first-rate. Dissatisfaction with the basic idea of a one-year course of world history was quite prevalent. In many of the schools I visited, a twelfth-grade course in American problems or American government was required of all students. In these courses a considerable amount of time was devoted to discussions of current topics. I was impressed, in a number of cases, with the success of these courses.

It should be emphasized that in the schools in which at least seven years of English and social studies are required of all, something approaching half the student's time is devoted to academic subjects even if he elects nonacademic courses for the rest of the program. In a sense, the judgment on the instruction in English and social studies is a judgment on the school's success in providing a solid academic background for all the future citizens of the community in question.

Item 3 reports on ability grouping, a highly controversial subject among administrators and teachers. I have marked with a plus sign those schools in which ability grouping was used in at least one subject. It was most commonly found in English, and usually instruction was given at three levels—one level for the top 10 to 15 per cent in terms of their ability in English, a second level for a large middle group, and a third for the very slow readers who often were handled by special teachers, as reported in Item 6 (special provision for slow readers).

Items 4 and 5 in Table 1 (adequate nonacademic elective programs and adequate opportunities for supervised work experience) represent my judgment on the elective programs which lead to the development of skills which the student may use in connection with a job immediately on graduation. In all the schools marked with a plus, two or more vocational programs were offered. These programs were organized either under the Smith–Hughes or George–Barden Acts, or they were financed locally but required essentially the same amount of time as the federally supported programs.

Advisory committees composed of representatives of labor and management are essential parts of an adequate vocational program. Such committees insure that programs correspond to the employment possibilities in the local community or area.

In judging Item 4, I had in mind not only programs for boys in the shops and, in a few cases, agricultural programs, but also the work offered for girls in stenography and office practice. To an outsider, this work would seem to be as much vocational as the development of skills in the shops by the boys. But in today's terminology the training of girls to be stenographers, office clerks, or office-machine operators is called a "commercial program" or "business training." In order to become a successful stenographer, a girl must pass the requisite courses with high standards over a period of at least two years. A course in typing must have been completed previously. For those who do not have the required ability to master stenography (and this subject requires more than average intellectual ability), courses in typing and clerical machine work may provide a meaningful elective program.

In many schools, those who were taking vocational courses were studying English and the social studies with all the other students; they were also sharing with other students the social experience of a homeroom and were taking part in the usual social and athletic activities of the school. In those schools which had satisfactory vocational programs, the administration of the school and the guidance officers did not treat them as "dumping grounds" for those of low academic ability. The vocational programs enrolled boys of at least average academic ability. The slow readers were excluded from the shops in which skilled trades were being taught.

I have marked Item 5 with a plus when the school had a work experience program organized as part of a student's high school program either with federal financial support or on a similar half-time-in-school and half-time-on-the-job basis, but financed locally. Under these programs, students in the eleventh and twelfth grades were placed in jobs (of a distributive or a diversified occupational nature, if the program is supported by federal funds) which occupied them for half a day and for which they received remuneration. They also studied at least one related academic course each term as part of their regular schoolwork. A program coordinator was usually charged with developing opportunities for employment in the community and with relating a student's school program to his employment.

Further information about vocational and work experience programs is given in Appendix F.

Item 6 is marked with a plus when a school had special arrangements for the education of those students whose reading ability was several grades below that of their classmates. The special provisions varied from school to school, but in essence they amounted to finding devoted and understanding teachers to work with this group and to provide instruction in the required subjects of a somewhat different nature from that offered to the rest of the student body. In some instances, steps were taken to direct the vocational orientation of the slow readers toward simple vocational work appropriate to their limited abilities.

Improvement of the reading ability of this group was, of course, of paramount importance, and work with remedial reading was provided. However, in the opinion of those involved in this difficult pedagogical task, it would be very difficult, even with the best of instruction, to raise the reading level of these students more than two grades, and only a few could reach the degree of efficiency that would enable them to enter regular classes in English and social studies later in their high school course.

Item 7 (special provisions for challenging the very able) is marked with a plus when a school either had special tutoring arrangements or offered at least one advanced placement course in the twelfth grade. The courses had to have been articulated with the program of some institution of higher learning. It was not necessary that they be organized under the aegis of the Advanced Placement Program.

Item 8 (special instruction in developing reading skills) indicates whether a school had a developmental reading program, an innovation that impressed me in some of the schools I visited. A school merited a plus for this item if the program was organized on a voluntary basis, if guidance counselors were successful in interesting bright students in the program, and if the requisite equipment was available.

Item 9 (regular summer session) requires only a brief comment. Where summer sessions were available only for remedial purposes and not for advanced work, I have not marked the school with a plus.

Item 10 (individualized programs) reports my findings in regard to the organization of the curriculum. Blank spaces in the table indicate that in the school in question there are definite programs with such labels as college preparatory, commercial, general, and vocational. In such schools a student enrolls in one of these programs in the ninth or tenth grade. His selection is quite well known throughout the school. Though electives are permitted, the pattern of courses tends to be determined by the program, particularly for those who elect the college-preparatory program.

The schools which we have indicated as having individualized programs are schools in which each pupil, with the aid of the counselor, determines his own elective program year by year. There may be suggested programs corresponding to different vocational interests, but the rigidity found in the other type of school is absent; furthermore, the pupils are less aware of their differentiation according to their interests and abilities than is the case in schools with definite programs or tracks.

Item 11 (school day organized into seven or more instructional periods) refers to the way in which the program of a school is organized, a matter of controversy among school administrators. A blank indicates a six-period day. In the schools I visited, the number of regular class periods in a day ranged from six, including periods for such required courses as physical education and driver training, to eight, plus another period for these nonacademic courses. The length of each period varied from forty to sixty minutes. In schools with shorter periods, laboratory and industrial arts classes were scheduled for two consecutive periods.

Item 12 records the basic facts about guidance in the schools we visited. If there were no guidance officers at all, or if there was only one full-time counselor for so many pupils as to make the possibility of effective work very slight, or if it seemed to me that counselors were inexperienced or untrained, I have left Item 15 blank. I have not attempted in this item to pass judgment on the effectiveness of the guidance service in steering the individual student into the program for which he is fitted by his ability, as demonstrated by tests and achievement in the courses. It would be extremely difficult without an exhaustive survey to pass such a judgment in regard to the nonacademic elective programs.

The next three items (Items 13, 14, and 15: good student morale, well-organized homerooms, effective social interaction) may be considered together.

To obtain evidence on which to judge student morale (Item 13), I had to rely largely on the students' responses to my questions and the opinions of the counselors and administrative officers, though the nature of the organization of the school was also of importance. As in the case of Items 1 and 2, my judgment might have been different if I could have stayed longer in the school. The same applies to Item 15 (effective social interaction).

The report on the existence or absence of well-organized homerooms (Item 14), on the other hand, is essentially factual. In some schools there were no homerooms or they were used merely as devices for disseminating administrative information to students each day. Opinions of principals and superintendents as to the effectiveness of homerooms varied enormously. I was impressed, however, by a few schools in which homerooms were organized in such a way as to provide adequate time for the work of the student council. In such schools, one or two representatives of each homeroom were elected to the student council and reported back to their constituency, so to speak,

what was going on in the student council. The effective homerooms on which I am reporting were heterogeneously grouped
—that is, students of varying abilities and different elective
programs were in the same room. The same homeroom group
was kept together for three or four years, so that a feeling of in-
timacy would develop among the students. I found schools
where the students' judgments as to the significance of the
homeroom reinforced what I had been told by the principal
concerning the importance of this phase of the schoolwork.

That there are other ways of developing an understanding
between students is clear from a comparison of Items 14 and
15; in a number of schools I visited an effective social interaction was present between students although there were either
no homerooms or homerooms did not seem to be well organized. The other ways of developing an understanding between
diverse types of students include, of course, participation in
programs of physical education and work in a variety of clubs.
Almost all of the schools I visited had a rather elaborate
series of clubs, but the opinion of the teachers, administrators,
and students varied from school to school as to the usefulness
and success of these activities.

Items 16 and 17 briefly summarize the academic inventory
which we obtained from the schools in question. As indicated
earlier in this report, the purpose of this inventory was to answer questions which no one in the schools could answer except
in very general terms. What I wanted to find out was whether
the able students were electing the stiff courses. From the
schools indicated, we obtained the program cards of the boys
and girls in the top 25 per cent of the class graduating in 1957
(without, of course, the names of students but with a designation of sex). The school indicated on each card what test was
employed and the score received. From this top 25 per cent,
we chose the top 15 per cent of the students, using for this
purpose the indicated test score. Different tests were used in
different schools, but they were all of the type called "scholastic aptitude tests" or "ability tests" and were designed to measure the ability of the student to handle academic studies.

I think it would be fair to say that the chances are good that few if any of those we included in the 15 per cent were students of merely average ability. On the other hand, we may well have missed a number of bright students in making up our 15-per cent group. Some schools provided grades on the programs sent to us, and these grades indicate that the members of the group we picked were in fact capable of handling mathematics, science, and foreign languages; the grades were, as a rule, *A* or *B*.

We then proceeded to examine the programs of each of these pupils, and the results are tabulated in full in Appendix D. It will be noted that we have included not only the elective programs but also the programs required by the local district or state. Most of the schools required four years of English of all the pupils. In the others, all the students were required to study English for at least three years. One can certainly question any program which omits the fourth year of English for able students. The consequence of such omission is certain to be serious, particularly as regards developing skill in writing.

Although in the majority of the schools the academically talented boys and girls had studied social studies for three years, there were a number of exceptions to this rule. I found only four schools in which a majority of the academically talented boys and girls were studying social studies for four years. In three quarters of the schools on which I am reporting, a majority of the academically talented students were studying English and social studies for a total of seven one-year courses. One cannot conclude, of course, that in three quarters of the thousands of comprehensive high schools of sufficient size in the United States an equally satisfactory situation prevails.

If one feels that at least the academically talented boys and girls should be studying a wide program which challenges their ability to the fullest, then seventeen or eighteen one-year courses of academic subjects would seem to be desirable; for example, seven years of English and social studies, seven years of mathematics and science, and four years' study of a foreign language. It will be seen that in schools *A, B, C, D,*

E, G, H, O, and *R* a majority of the academically talented *boys* had elected a program with seventeen or more academic subjects a year in four years.

It is interesting that the election of art and music (two subjects which do not require homework as a rule, and, therefore, subjects I have *not* listed as academic subjects) was high even in the school with the most extensive inventory (school *C*), whereas in school *V*, in which the academic inventory for boys was highly unsatisfactory, the election of art and music was scanty. In this connection I would refer the reader back to what was said a few paragraphs earlier in regard to our findings reported in Item 11 (periods in the school day). The relatively small percentage of the academically talented boys electing two years of art and music in schools *H, N, Q, T,* and *V* may be in part accounted for by the fact that in these schools there is a six-period day.

Those who are directly concerned with the determination of policy for, or the administration of, high schools will perhaps wish to scrutinize Table 1 with considerable care. The qualifications I have stated earlier in regard to the firmness of the judgments expressed by certain of the items must be remembered. Even allowing for the uncertainties, I was interested to see if there appeared to be any incompatibility between those procedures and types of organization I considered satisfactory and the school's exhibiting a fairly satisfactory academic inventory (Items 16d and 17d—at least seventeen full academic subjects). Furthermore, I was curious as to the relation of certain of the first fifteen items in Table 1 to each other. For example, it is quite evident that with the exception of school *M*, there appeared to be satisfactory social interaction among all the students (Item 15) in all the schools where we found well-organized homerooms (Item 14), but that in several schools (*D, E, I, N, O, P, S*) there appeared to be effective social interaction without any organized homerooms. The small size of the school and the homogeneity of the school population explain the situation in school *O*. The other cases are evidence that, as mentioned earlier, other methods besides homerooms may be effective in promoting an understanding between students with different vocational orientations. Furthermore, it must be remembered that Item 15 measures a resultant of the force generated by the school on behalf of social integration and the forces in the community which may work in the other direction. It would really be unfair to compare two schools in this respect without knowing a great deal about the socioeconomic stratification of the communities in question.

At first sight it might appear that if Item 7 (challenge to the very able) is satisfactory, the academic inventory should also be satisfactory, but this conclusion does not necessarily follow. In Item 7, I am reporting on special ways in which the top 2 or 3 per cent of the student body were challenged, a group often referred to as the highly gifted. Adequate provisions were found in a number of schools which showed an unsatisfactory academic inventory; for example, schools *U* and *V*. It is clear that concern for the very top group does not automatically insure that all the academically talented will be stimulated to elect a full program.

It is sometimes said that no school can be interested in both the academically talented and those at the opposite end of the scholastic spectrum. Comparison of Item 6 (special provision for the slow reader) with 7 (special provision for challenging the very able) shows that this was not the case in a number of schools I visited. (Note schools *C, D, E, F, I, K, L, M*, and *V*.)

The fact that school *C* has such a highly satisfactory inventory and yet has clearly defined separate programs (a blank on Item 10) might be taken as evidence that the academically talented would only elect a full program if they were placed in a fairly rigid academic or college-preparatory program or track. But the information on schools *A* and *B* shows that this conclusion does not always hold. Furthermore, it is quite clear that in a number of other schools which have individualized programs (such as schools *D, E, F, G*, and *H*) a small change would have brought these schools into the same category as schools *A* and *B*. This change would have been brought about, I feel sure, if the administration and the counselors had emphasized the importance of the study of one foreign language for at least four years. *Indeed, it is interesting that in nine schools we examined, 50 per cent or more of the academically talented boys had taken seventeen academic subjects in four years, and in ten schools, a few, at least, had taken as many as nineteen.* These figures show that Recommendation 9 (p. 57), insofar as the number of courses with homework is concerned, is quite possible; it corresponds with what I have found in certain schools. Indeed, one can conclude from an examination of these tables that there is no reason why in a given school all the Items 1 through 15 should not be marked with a plus sign and why the plus signs in Items 16 and 17 (the academic inventory) should not appear as frequently for all schools as for schools *A*, *B*, and *C*.

Tables D1 and D2 give the detailed information obtained from
the academic inventories of the twenty-two schools listed in
Table 1 (p. 24). Items 16 and 17 in Table 1 are a summary of
the data given in more detail in Tables D1 and D2, which
follow.

As explained in Appendix H, an academic inventory
should be based on the results of scholastic aptitude tests given
in grades seven, eight, or nine, and the upper 15 per cent should
be chosen on the basis of a *national norm*. In a number of the
schools, the tests were given in higher grades, and to the extent
that this fact tends to introduce a complicating factor, some of
the inventories may be in error. Different schools used different
tests, but we believe we have been able to relate them all to a
national norm. The test scores of the bottom of the 15 per
cent whose programs are summarized in the tables were about
115 on a scale in which the national norm is 100. Because the
mean I.Q. of the pupils in all the schools from which we obtained data was about the same (100 to 106), the top 15 per
cent of the graduating class as measured by aptitude tests in each
school would be comparable with each other.

Since we asked each school for the programs of the boys
and girls who stood in the upper 25 per cent on the basis of a
scholastic aptitude or intelligence test, we had at our disposal
a considerable amount of information in addition to that given
in the tables. A survey of the programs of those whose test
scores placed them just outside the 15 per cent group showed
little variation from the pattern of courses elected by the
top 15 per cent in the school in question. This similarity is,
of course, what would be expected. There is no hard and fast
line between those I have designated academically talented
and those with lesser abilities as measured by a test score. The
upper 25 per cent tend to elect about the same programs as
the upper 15 per cent in a given school, but as one passes to
students with lower and lower scores, the programs tend to
become less rigorous. Tests being imperfect, undoubtedly there
were in each school some in the 15 to 25 per cent group who

TABLE D1: *Academic Inventory Summary—Boys**

Schools	Total No. of A. T. Boys in Class	Math Years		Science Years			Combination of Math and Science Years				Eng. Years	Social Studies Years		
		3	4	2	3	4	5	6	7	8	4	2	3	4
A	7	100	15	70	70	55	70	70	55	15	100	100	100	15
B	30	95	60	95	80	45	90	90	60	35	100	100	45	10
C	53	85	55	90	85	65	85	85	65	55	100	100	100	100
D	25	90	65	90	80	50	90	80	70	35	100	100	90	5
E	10	100	100	100	100	70	100	100	100	70	100	100	20	10
F	28	70	55	100	85	20	95	70	55	15	100	100	100	20
G	7	100	100	100	85	55	100	100	85	55	100	100	100	30
H	12	100	90	85	60	25	90	85	60	25	100	100	100	15
I	32	95	75	95	70	20	95	90	60	15	55	100	55	10
J	25	90	70	75	50	15	90	65	50	10	95	100	100	55
K	26	70	60	95	80	35	90	70	55	30	95	100	100	25
L	35	90	80	75	50	10	90	70	50	5	100	100	75	20
M	40	65	60	90	65	25	80	70	50	15	100	100	95	5
N	48	85	60	70	55	10	75	60	50	10	65	100	80	25
O	6	85	35	100	65	—	85	65	35	—	100	100	100	85
P	12	65	60	75	40	25	65	60	50	15	90	100	100	—
Q	14	95	70	100	95	55	95	95	80	50	50	100	100	30
R	20	85	70	100	75	30	95	95	55	25	85	100	20	—
S	20	90	75	80	10	—	85	75	5	—	60	100	100	25
T	29	90	80	95	75	20	90	85	60	15	95	100	25	5
U	28	55	35	95	50	25	70	45	30	10	100	100	100	100
V	47	65	45	70	40	—	70	55	25	—	35	100	30	20

* Numbers indicate the percentage of Academically Talented Boys. All numbers have been rounded off to the nearest 5 per cent.

114

Combination of Eng. and Soc. Studies Years			Foreign Lang. Years					Art and Music Years		Total Academic Subjects				
6	7	8	2	3	4	5	6	1	2	15	16	17	18	19
100	100	15	70	70	70	—	—	85	55	70	70	70	55	55
100	50	20	95	60	35	15	5	30	15	100	85	65	35	15
100	100	100	85	70	55	—	—	100	85	100	90	90	85	70
100	90	5	70	30	20	15	10	50	40	75	65	50	20	10
100	20	10	90	70	20	20	—	60	20	100	100	80	20	—
100	100	30	75	50	50	—	—	65	45	85	70	45	30	15
100	100	30	100	30	15	—	—	70	45	100	85	70	30	—
100	100	60	60	10	—	—	—	50	15	100	85	65	25	15
75	35	5	90	50	15	—	—	55	30	70	65	35	5	5
100	100	50	50	15	10	—	—	65	45	70	50	25	10	—
100	100	50	40	—	—	—	—	60	40	70	35	20	—	—
100	70	20	65	30	15	5	—	65	45	65	45	20	5	—
100	95	10	80	10	5	—	—	80	50	75	40	10	5	—
95	75	35	70	20	10	—	—	35	20	65	50	15	10	5
100	100	85	85	—	—	—	—	65	35	85	65	65	15	—
100	90	10	25	—	—	—	—	50	25	25	15	—	—	—
100	55	15	65	—	—	—	—	30	15	70	55	30	5	—
85	30	—	95	40	35	—	—	60	40	85	85	50	20	—
100	70	30	55	30	15	—	—	45	25	45	35	30	15	—
95	35	10	85	10	—	—	—	20	5	80	45	15	5	—
100	100	100	45	5	5	—	—	40	25	65	40	30	15	5
50	25	15	65	20	—	—	—	20	10	40	15	5	5	5

TABLE D2: *Academic Inventory Summary—Girls**

Schools	Total No. of A. T. Girls in Class	Math Years		Science Years			Combination of Math and Science Years				Eng. Years	Social Studies Years		
		3	4	2	3	4	5	6	7	8	4	2	3	4
A	7	85	—	100	70	45	85	70	45	—	100	100	85	—
B	26	75	15	70	15	—	60	25	5	5	100	100	15	—
C	61	80	20	80	75	25	80	75	35	10	100	100	100	95
D	33	60	25	80	50	5	70	50	20	5	100	100	100	10
E	17	70	35	90	65	25	80	60	40	10	100	100	40	—
F	62	30	5	85	30	5	45	15	5	—	95	100	100	10
G	21	60	25	85	60	10	65	50	30	5	100	100	100	15
H	48	40	5	45	10	5	25	10	5	5	100	100	100	10
I	32	25	—	65	25	5	45	10	—	—	80	100	55	30
J	29	40	20	50	30	5	45	20	10	—	95	100	100	75
K	34	15	10	85	20	5	30	20	—	—	90	100	100	55
L	25	70	35	55	15	—	50	30	5	—	95	100	90	30
M	21	10	5	65	5	—	15	5	—	—	100	100	65	—
N	34	25	10	60	35	5	45	20	5	—	60	100	90	25
O	5	40	40	100	40	—	60	40	20	—	100	100	100	100
P	5	—	—	60	—	—	—	—	—	—	100	100	100	20
Q	25	15	5	100	70	30	70	35	10	5	80	100	100	40
R	40	55	10	85	55	5	75	40	10	5	90	100	40	5
S	27	30	15	60	10	—	35	20	—	—	70	100	100	20
T	42	50	25	85	65	30	75	50	25	15	90	100	10	5
U	32	25	5	100	40	10	45	20	15	5	100	100	100	100
V	44	15	5	50	20	5	25	5	5	—	70	100	35	15

* Numbers indicate the percentage of Academically Talented Girls. All numbers have been rounded off to the nearest 5 per cent.

Combination of Eng. and Soc. Studies Years			Foreign Lang. Years					Art and Music Years		Total Academic Subjects				
6	7	8	2	3	4	5	6	1	2	15	16	17	18	19
100	85	—	100	70	55	15	—	100	85	85	85	55	30	15
95	35	10	100	95	90	75	10	55	25	90	90	60	35	15
100	100	95	80	75	85	5	—	100	100	80	80	80	75	50
100	100	5	75	50	35	20	—	25	20	65	55	35	25	10
100	40	5	100	90	65	55	10	80	75	100	95	80	10	—
100	95	25	80	55	55	—	—	95	70	60	60	35	15	5
100	100	60	75	35	35	—	—	85	85	65	60	45	15	5
100	100	35	65	20	15	10	—	75	45	35	30	15	—	—
90	65	35	80	40	5	—	—	60	35	55	30	15	5	—
100	95	75	95	50	25	10	5	90	60	75	50	25	5	5
100	100	70	50	5	5	—	—	75	65	40	20	10	—	—
95	90	30	90	60	50	5	5	90	85	60	45	20	5	—
100	65	5	95	50	15	—	—	80	65	10	5	—	—	—
100	65	40	90	40	30	—	—	65	40	40	35	20	5	5
100	100	100	40	—	—	—	—	100	100	100	80	20	—	—
100	100	40	20	—	—	—	—	100	60	40	—	—	—	—
100	90	40	55	10	5	—	—	70	30	45	25	10	5	—
95	55	25	90	65	55	—	—	80	65	75	55	25	5	—
100	75	35	75	50	15	—	—	75	50	50	20	10	5	—
90	15	10	85	30	10	5	—	70	40	50	35	15	5	5
100	100	100	55	5	—	—	—	80	45	40	30	25	10	5
80	45	20	70	40	5	—	—	55	35	20	5	—	—	—

should have been included in the top 15 per cent. These students would have affected the figures given in the tables little, however, because their programs were similar to those of students in the top 15 per cent.

It is hardly necessary to warn the reader against attempting any generalizations based on the data in Tables D1 and D2. The twenty-two schools reported are by no means a random sample of American high schools. All the schools (except two) were of sufficient size (graduating classes of one hundred or more), all were widely comprehensive (as compared with suburban schools), all had a good reputation. It would be quite fallacious, for example, to assume that because in two of these schools a majority of the academically talented boys had elected programs with at least nineteen academic subjects, the academic inventories of something like 10 per cent of the high schools in the nation would reveal a similar situation. The only way to determine what in fact the academically talented youth are studying in the approximately four thousand high schools of sufficient size throughout the country would be to compile an academic inventory *for each school*. A start has been made in this direction by the State of Maryland.

Appendix E: MARYLAND ACADEMIC INVENTORY

The state of Maryland has led the way in providing meaningful information about the degree to which able students in each high school of sufficient size in the state are being challenged intellectually and the degree to which these students are responding to the challenge by electing a wide academic program of stiff courses. An academic inventory of all students testing at 120 I.Q. and above in those 1958 Maryland high school graduating classes which had at least one hundred students was made by the Maryland State Department of Education. The inventory was one phase of a comprehensive study of backgrounds, intellectual abilities, courses and subjects pursued, interests, and future plans of all 1958 graduates.

The results of the academic inventory reveal some interesting facts about individual high schools in Maryland. One can generalize about the proportion of these schools that are handling their academically talented students well in certain respects, but one cannot thereby generalize about the state's secondary system as a whole.

There are 147 public senior high schools in Maryland. Only fifty-two (35 per cent) have graduating classes of at least one hundred and were thus included in the academic inventory. Since it is believed that smaller schools cannot adequately provide for the bright student, they were not included. Of the fifty-two high schools studied, there were forty-five high schools in which there were academically talented boys and forty-six in which there were academically talented girls.

Involved in the inventory were 1245 students—741 boys and 504 girls. The small high schools which were excluded—some 95 in number—enrolled only 129 academically talented youngsters. Thus, the inventory included more than 90 per cent of the students who tested at 120 and above.

Two general comments must be made in approaching the results. In the first place, individual schools vary enormously in the degree to which they are able to guide their academically talented students into tough courses. Secondly, all schools would have a far more satisfactory record if more of the able students were studying three or more years of a foreign language.

However, the recent furor about our public schools has concerned mathematics and science, and not foreign languages. It is, therefore, important to note the generally good record with regard to boys made by Maryland high schools in these fields. At least seven years of mathematics and science were studied by virtually all the more able boys in eleven high schools (24 per cent of the schools), by at least three quarters of these boys in seventeen schools (almost 40 per cent of the schools), and by at least half of the more able boys in forty schools (almost 90 per cent of the high schools).

The more able girls are not nearly so well represented in mathematics and science classes. At least seven years of these subjects were studied by virtually all the more able girls in only five high schools (11 per cent of the schools), and by at least one half of the more able girls in only fifteen high schools (33 per cent of the schools). One cannot avoid the conclusion that some Maryland high schools, by allowing their academically talented girls to avoid studying advanced mathematics and science, are depriving the state of many future teachers in these important fields where there is already a critical shortage of qualified teachers.

The even more serious problem is in the foreign language field. Very few of the more able students of either sex are studying enough foreign language. The typical pattern of foreign language study in Maryland is two years of one language. At least three years of one language are studied by no more than two thirds of the more able girls and one half of the more able boys in any high school. This record is achieved in only a few of the schools—in three of those with girls and in two of those with boys. Half of the more able girls studied at least three years of one language in only four of the high schools.

At least two years of one foreign language were studied by virtually all of the more able girls in twenty-seven high schools (59 per cent of the schools), by at least three quarters of these girls in thirty-six high schools (78 per cent of the schools), and by at least half of the more able girls in forty-one high schools (89 per cent of the schools).

At least two years of one foreign language were studied

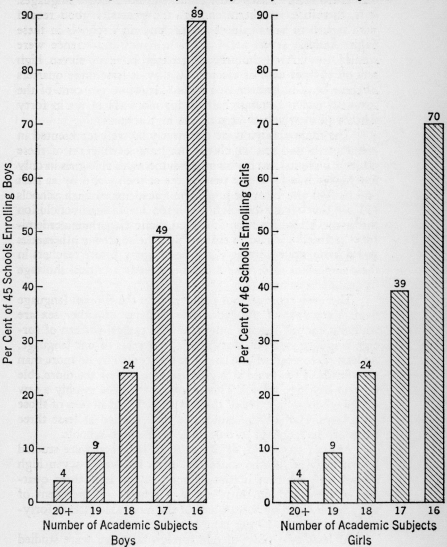

DIAGRAM A

Number of Academic Subjects Taken by at Least 75 Per Cent of the More Able Boys and Girls during Four High School Years, as Shown by Inventory of 1958 Graduating Classes

Boys (Per Cent of 45 Schools Enrolling Boys)

Number of Academic Subjects	Per Cent
20+	4
19	9
18	24
17	49
16	89

Girls (Per Cent of 46 Schools Enrolling Girls)

Number of Academic Subjects	Per Cent
20+	4
19	9
18	24
17	39
16	70

by virtually all of the more able boys in twenty high schools (38 per cent of the schools), by at least three quarters of these boys in thirty-eight high schools (85 per cent of the schools), and by at least half of the more able boys in virtually all of the high schools.

Diagram A on the preceding page presents a summary of the number of courses elected by three-quarters of the more able students in the fifty-two schools. It is interesting that there are a number of comprehensive high schools in the State of Maryland in which three-quarters of the more able boys and girls have taken as many as nineteen subjects with homework and a few schools in which the programs of the same type of student included twenty or more subjects with homework. In these schools, a far larger percentage of the more able students had elected a really wide program of academic subjects than in any of the twenty-two schools listed in Appendix D. I am indebted to Dr. Thomas G. Pullen, State Superintendent, for making available the data from which the academic inventories could be compiled.

Appendix F: VOCATIONAL EDUCATION*

Definition: The term *vocational education* as used in this report applies to work at the high school level for which funds are provided under the national vocational education acts of 1917 (Smith–Hughes) and 1946 (George–Barden) or to work similarly organized but operating without federal assistance. Federal funds must be matched with state and/or local public funds. Federal funds are made available to state boards for vocational education (created by state laws) for salaries and travel of directors, supervisors, teacher-trainers, and salaries of vocational teachers under the provisions of the above-mentioned acts. The present national pattern for meeting the cost of vocational education programs is as follows: four dollars contributed by the states for every one dollar from the federal government. It should be noted that federal money supports both high school and adult programs and that there is a slight majority of the latter. Only high school programs are considered in this report.

Aim: The controlling purpose of vocational education programs at the high school level is to develop skills for useful employment. These programs relate schoolwork to a specific occupational goal but involve more than training for specific job skills.

Vocational education is not offered in lieu of general academic education, but grows out of it, supplementing and enhancing it. Vocational education is an integral part of the total education program and requires aptitude that students at the lowest academic level do not have. Slow readers, for example, are not able to benefit from regular vocational programs.

Operation: Each state has a Director of Vocational Education or the equivalent as part of its Department of Education. For the most part, vocational education programs are operated as part of the curriculum in comprehensive high schools. In

---

* This appendix is based upon material published by the Division of Vocational Education of the United States Office of Education (especially pamphlet No. 117, *Public Vocational Education Programs*) and upon interviews with staff members of the Division and of the American Vocational Association.

Connecticut, Wisconsin, and Massachusetts, however, vocational education is provided only in separate vocational schools, and in many of the larger cities in other states such schools have been established.

Types of Program: The following types of program are included in vocational education:

A. Trade and Industrial (T & I)
The major objective of trade and industrial education is to provide instruction of a preparatory type in the development of basic manipulative skills, safety judgment, technical knowledge, and related industrial information for the purpose of fitting persons for useful employment in trades and industrial pursuits.

This objective is attained through various types of program. Each program is specific in purpose and is designed to serve the training needs of individual industrial workers. Training programs may be organized to provide instruction in:

1. Any industrial pursuit, skilled or semiskilled trade, craft, or occupation which directly functions in the designing, producing, processing, assembling, maintaining, servicing, or repairing of any manufactured product.
2. Any service trade or occupation which is not classified as agricultural, business, professional, or homemaking.
3. Other occupations which are usually considered as technical and in which workers such as nurses, laboratory assistants, draftsmen, and technicians are employed.

T & I programs are generally limited to the last two years of high school. A student usually takes industrial arts courses before enrolling in a T & I program.

For an effective T & I program, a school must be large enough to support a full-time director. At least four different trades would have to be included—machine shop, woodwork shop, auto mechanics shop, and electrical shop. The requirements of such an operation have sometimes led to the development of area vocational programs in high schools. These programs include students from several school districts. The state usually pays the transportation cost.

More important even than the size of the school are the type of community and the occupational setup within it. A T & I program is costly, and a school board generally is not interested unless the community can employ the graduates. An advisory committee composed of local businessmen, labor leaders, and community leaders is essential.

The Smith–Hughes Act prescribes a six-hour day for T & I pupils in grades eleven and twelve. Three are spent in the shop and three in general education subjects, including at least one subject each term related to the vocational program; e.g., mathematics, mechanical drawing, science.

B. Distributive Education
Distributive education programs prepare students for occupations followed by workers directly engaged in merchandising activities, or in contact with buyers and sellers when:

1. Distributing to consumers, retailers, jobbers, wholesalers, and others the products of farm and industry, or selling services.
2. Managing, operating, or conducting a retail, wholesale, or service business.

This program is often called the work experience program. During the eleventh and twelfth grades, pupils work on a regular job no less than fifteen hours per week for which they receive remuneration.

As in the other programs, one course each term must be devoted to a related subject.

C. Home Economics
The controlling purpose of vocational education is "to fit

for useful employment"; hence it follows that the controlling purpose of vocational education in home economics, as provided for by the vocational education acts, is to prepare for the responsibilities and activities involved in homemaking and in achieving family well-being. The general objective of vocational education in home economics is to provide instruction which will enable families to improve the quality of their family life through the more efficient development and utilization of human and material resources. Vocational programs, therefore, need to provide for instruction in all of the aspects of home living and homemaking. A student is enrolled throughout her high school career.

D. Agriculture

The purpose of vocational education in agriculture is to increase proficiency in farming. Students are enrolled in vocational agriculture programs throughout their high school course. For at least six months of the year, students must have access to farms where they are permitted full responsibility for carrying out programs under a teacher's guidance. In actual practice, most of these programs are carried out on a year-round basis, the students working on them on Saturdays and in the afternoons after school. Students must also take one course related to the program as a regular part of their academic schedule.

Vocational agriculture also includes, as an extracurricular activity, training in the civic and professional aspects of a farmer's life. The Future Farmers of America (F.F.A.) is open to any boy in the program. The F.F.A. tries to provide experience in leadership (public speaking, etc.) and in management (running a cooperative, etc.).

E. Practical Nursing

This program operates as a section in a trade and industrial program.

F. Fishing (Commercial)

This new program is divided between the trade and industrial and the distributive education programs. For the most part, it is being set up for adults and not at the high school level.

Comments: In the first place, anything that is said or written on the subject of vocational education must be considered in connection with the state in which the high school is located. As noted above, the administration of the federally aided vocational programs varies from state to state.

My inclination is strongly in favor of including vocational work in a comprehensive high school instead of providing it in a separate high school. My reasons are largely social rather than educational. I believe it is important for the future of American democracy to have as close a relationship as possible in high school between the future professional man, the future craftsman, the future manager of industry, the future labor leader, the future salesman, and the future engineer. As I have often stressed in my writings and earlier in this report, I am convinced that one of the fundamental doctrines of American society is equality of status in all forms of honest labor as well as equality of opportunity.

To my mind, it is desirable for as many boys and girls in high school as possible to have an ultimate vocational goal. It may well be that many of them will change their minds before the high school course is over or in later years. But, if a student thinks that what he or she is studying in school is likely to have significance in later life, the study in question takes on a new importance. There is less tendency for such "committed" students to waste their time or have a negative attitude toward their schoolwork.

Analysis of Enrollments: The following table (Table F1) presents data pertaining to vocational education in twenty-one states. The students who are included in this tabulation may be enrolled either in a comprehensive high school or a separate vocational school.

It is interesting to note the wide variations in the percentage of the youth enrolled in vocational courses supported by

	No. of High Schs.	(1)Enrol., grades 9–12	(2)Enrol., Voc. Ag. (male)	Per Cent of Males Voc. Ag.	(1)Enrol., grades 11 & 12	(3)Enrol., T. & I. (male)	(4)Enrol., D. E. (male)	Per Cent of 11th- and 12th-grade males, T. & I. and D. E.
California	481	452,076	13,373	5.9	184,589	17,382	604	19.5
Connecticut	100	69,108	533	1.5	29,395	4,719	51	32.5
Delaware	34	12,365	890	14.4	5,148	822	107	36.1
Illinois	693	319,580	16,754	10.5	140,756	6,072	535	9.4
Indiana	824	185,551	12,476	13.4	77,719	3,582	233	9.8
Iowa	745	123,477	11,728	19.0	55,401	2,187	158	8.5
Kansas	636	93,531	6,652	14.2	41,622	1,506	139	7.9
Maryland	147	84,640	3,249	7.7	33,464	5,341	143	32.8
Massachusetts	242	169,734	1,335	1.6	73,896	13,806	180	37.9
Michigan	512	265,355	12,421	9.4	116,269	7,206	1,211	14.5
Minnesota	519	138,570	12,901	18.6	61,729	3,299	195	11.3
Missouri	555	154,815	11,733	15.2	65,604	3,705	1,016	14.4
New Jersey	170	170,589	1,563	1.8	72,270	4,242	123	12.1
New York	968	526,483	4,484	1.7	221,759	25,272	1,482	24.1
Ohio	958	328,570	11,432	7.0	137,151	4,691	325	7.3
Oregon	224	75,819	3,889	10.3	32,258	1,684	232	11.9
Pennsylvania	822	430,530	11,916	5.5	182,802	17,397	514	19.6
Rhode Island	29	20,608	347	3.4	8,908	1,265	—	28.4
Texas	1,198	335,404	43,781	26.1	136,102	7,998	2,790	15.9
Washington	291	106,868	7,919	14.8	46,132	4,730	279	21.7
Wisconsin	420	149,570	16,615	22.2	67,433	2,592	—	7.7

(1) Enrollment, by grade, in full-time public secondary schools. 1953–54 *Biennial Report*, U.S. Office of Education. The total figure is divided on a 50-50 basis for boys and girls.

(2) Enrollment in all-day Vocational Agriculture classes, fiscal year, 1956. *Digest of Annual Reports of State Boards for Vocational Education*, U.S. Office of Education.

Vocational Education Programs in High Schools in Certain States

(5)Enrol., Home Ec. (male)	Total Voc. Enrol. (male)	(5)Enrol., Home Ec. (female)	Per Cent in Home Ec. (female)	(3)Enrol., T. & I. (female)	(4)Enrol., D. E. (female)	Per Cent of 11th- and 12th-grade in T. & I. and D. E. (female)	Per Cent in Voc. Programs (excluding Home Ec.) (male)	Per Cent in Voc. Programs (female)
1,085	32,444	38,820	17.2	5,138	568	6.2	25.4	23.4
264	5,565	3,537	10.2	627	94	4.9	34.0	15.1
—	1,819	2,673	43.2	181	98	10.8	50.5	54.0
1,125	24,486	34,851	21.8	1,229	626	2.6	19.9	41.7
531	16,822	29,277	31.6	261	246	1.3	23.2	32.9
164	14,237	14,754	23.9	238	212	1.8	27.5	25.7
451	8,748	10,443	22.3	60	159	1.1	22.1	23.4
1	8,734	2,951	7.0	1,277	315	9.5	40.5	16.5
—	15,321	2,461	2.9	1,371	158	4.1	39.5	7.0
1,651	22,489	30,114	22.7	1,684	1,247	5.0	23.9	29.7
265	16,660	16,899	23.4	853	221	3.5	29.9	26.9
336	16,790	18,156	23.5	1,217	627	5.6	29.6	29.1
586	6,514	1,797	2.1	346	123	1.3	13.9	3.4
—	31,238	13,367	5.1	8,670	1,944	9.6	25.8	14.7
—	16,448	15,428	9.4	1,535	539	3.0	14.3	12.4
—	5,805	5,715	15.1	431	321	4.7	22.2	19.8
74	29,901	15,414	7.2	3,061	730	4.1	25.1	11.3
—	1,612	1,368	13.3	109	—	2.4	31.8	15.7
2,809	57,378	80,572	48.0	3,156	2,313	8.0	42.0	56.0
826	13,754	22,842	42.7	1,542	395	8.4	36.5	51.1
71	19,278	12,176	16.3	565	—	1.7	29.9	18.0

(3) Enrollment in all-day and part-time Cooperative (Diversified Occupations) Vocational Trade and Industrial Classes, fiscal year, 1956. *Ibid.*

(4) Enrollment in part-time Cooperative Vocational Distributive Occupations (Distributive Education) Classes, fiscal year, 1956. *Ibid.*

(5) Enrollment in all-day Vocational Home Economics Classes, fiscal year, 1956. *Ibid.*

federal money. It will be evident that the percentage of the boys taking nonagricultural vocational work at the high school level varies by fivefold between Ohio (7.3 per cent) and Delaware (36.1 per cent). The percentage enrolled in vocational agriculture programs varies even more: the minimum is in Connecticut (1.5 per cent); the maximum (26.1 per cent), in Texas. These variations would seem to be correlated with the extent to which agriculture is important in the economy of the state. The variations in the percentage in the trade and industrial and the distributive education programs, however, would seem to reflect decisions of educational authorities, for there seems no obvious correlation between the figures and the degree of industrialization of the state.

Far more significant data would be supplied by the breakdown of these figures school by school. This information, however, appears not to be available in a compiled form.

Appendix G: **FORTY-EIGHT STATE SUMMARY OF THE NUMBER OF PUBLIC HIGH SCHOOLS AND TWELFTH-GRADE ENROLLMENTS**

[Pages 132, 133]

State	Year	Estimated Total No. 12th-Grade Students	12th-Grade Students in Schools with 12th-Grade Enrollment of Less Than 100		Total No. Schools Offering Diplomas	Schools Offering Diploma with 12th-Grade Enrollment of Less Than 100	
			Est. Number	Est. Per Cent		Est. Number	Est. Per Cent
Alabama[a]	1956–57	28,659	19,151	67	534	487	91
Arizona[a]	1956–57	8,864	1,937	22	83	62	75
Arkansas[a]	1956–57	16,802	12,370	73	491	468	95
California	1956–57	139,597[d]	7,139[d]	5.1	481[c]	148[a]	30.8
Colorado[a]	1957–58	13,304	3,181	24	267	218	82
Connecticut[b]	1955–56	15,080	2,440	16	100	39	39
Delaware[a]	1956–57	2,950	1,165	39	34	25	76.4
Florida[a]	1957–58	30,321	7,658	25	312	214	68.5
Georgia[c]	1955–56	UNAVAILABLE			667	UNAVAILABLE	
Idaho[a]	1957–58	7,832	3,460	44	127	107	84
Illinois[b]	1956–57	78,531	18,201	23.2	693	487	70.3
Indiana[b]	1955–56	46,388	18,563	40	824[c]	643[c]	78
Iowa[b]	1957–58	29,430	17,658	60	745	714	96
Kansas[b]	1957–58	25,293	12,928	51.1	636	586	92.1
Kentucky[b]	1957–58	22,860	14,835	65	423	386	91
Louisiana[a]	1957–58	24,649	14,028	56.9	496	447	90
Maine[a]	1957–58	8,981	4,276	47	170	152	89
Maryland[b]	1955–56	15,163	3,963	26	147[a]	95[a]	65
Massachusetts[b]	1956–57	40,360	6,092	15	242	98	40
Michigan[b]	1956–57	57,660	17,260	30	512	369	72
Minnesota[b]	1957–58	48,210	23,210	48.1	519	428	82.5
Mississippi[a]	1956–57	13,740	10,929	79.5	449	431	96
Missouri[b]	1957–58	39,424	18,285	46.4	555	495	87.4
Montana[a]	1956–57	6,333	915	14.5	171	94	55
Nebraska[a]	1957–58	14,000	8,267	59	438	421	96.1
Nevada[a]	1957–58	1,845	716	38.8	36	30	83.3
New Hampshire[a]	1957–58	4,139	2,100	50	80	69	86
New Jersey[b]	1955–56	36,020	1,920	6	170	28	16
New Mexico[a]	1956–57	7,270	2,038	28	106	75	70.7
New York[b]	1954–55	131,508	17,269	13	968	506	52

High Schools and 12th-Grade Enrollments

State	Year	Estimated Total No. 12th-Grade Students	12th-Grade Students in Schools with 12th-Grade Enrollment of Less Than 100		Total No. Schools Offering Diplomas	Schools Offering Diploma with 12th-Grade Enrollment of Less Than 100	
			Est. Number	Est. Per Cent		Est. Number	Est. Per Cent
North Carolina[a]	1956–57	41,474	34,000	81	848	790	93
North Dakota[a]	1956–57	6,517	5,214	80	352	345	98
Ohio[b]	1956–57	93,800	32,000	34	958	684	72
Oklahoma[a]	1956–57	25,741	13,950	54	656	617	94
Oregon[b]	1956–57	18,259	6,300	34.5	224	175	78.1
Pennsylvania[b]	1955–56	152,590	21,190	14	822	408	48
Rhode Island[a]	1957–58	4,597	681	14	29	12	41
South Carolina[a]	1957–58	19,904	13,677	68.5	360	321	89
South Dakota[a]	1957–58	7,167	5,419	75	261	253	96
Tennessee[a]	1956–57	29,181	17,550	60	442	351	79
Texas[b]	1955–56	70,588	9,557	13.5	1,198	700	58.4
Utah[a]	1956–57	9,923	1,954	20	78	49	63
Vermont[a]	1957–58	3,131	2,095	67	79	74	93.6
Virginia[a]	1956–57	24,312	11,606	47	393	277	73
Washington[b]	1956–57	23,388	8,050	34.4	291	231	79.4
West Virginia[a]	1956–57	20,646	8,574	41	374	185	50
Wisconsin[b]	1956–57	38,481	14,446	37.5	420	340	81
Wyoming[a]	1956–57	3,295	1,825	55	85	77	90
Total for Public High Schools in 26 States Included in Study		1,179,667	290,488	24.6	11,656	8,188	70.2
Total for Public Schools in the United States		1,507,027	478,542	31.8	19,194[f]	14,184	73.9[e]

[a] Figures provided by Chief State School Officers.
[b] Figures compiled from latest available report of Chief State School Officers.
[c] Figures provided by U.S. Office of Education.
[d] Figures provided by California Teachers Association.
[e] Percentage is based on total number of schools offering diplomas less those in Georgia, from which information concerning the number of small high schools was not available.
[f] The figure 21,000 used throughout this report is the latest information from the U.S. Office of Education.

Appendix H: INSTRUCTIONS FOR PREPARATION
OF AN ACADEMIC INVENTORY*

The academic inventory is a factual report. The only judgments expressed are those involved in determining the criteria for identifying the academically talented and in applying these criteria. However, the school board and the administrative officers, as well as the teaching staff, may have formulated a policy in regard to what this group of students ought to study. The results of the inventory in such a case can be matched against the recommended courses or programs, and the evidence will show to what extent this group of students have elected the courses recommended by the school (see p. 57).

Setting the Criteria: A statistical definition of the academically talented student is of critical importance in a study of this kind and must be reached with a great deal of care. Such a statistical definition has been accomplished in the following way by a number of schools:

A. From the student folders of last year's graduating class, list the name of every student who in grades seven, eight, or nine earned a score on a scholastic aptitude or intelligence test more than *one standard deviation above the mean.* This score is equal to the eighty-fourth percentile rank. If the test score is reported as an intelligence quotient (I.Q.), the score one standard deviation above the mean will be about 115, but the manual for the test should be consulted to find the exact standard deviation in I.Q. points, which should be added to 100 to obtain the cutting score. If the test score is reported as a standard score (a derivative of the standard deviation), the manual for the test will tell which score is one standard deviation above the mean of the norming group.

B. To this list of students with high scores on tests of academic aptitude add the names of other students, regardless of

* A condensation of a manual published by The Educational Testing Service, Princeton, New Jersey.

scholastic aptitude test scores, who in the ninth grade received high honor grades (90–100, *A*— or *A*) in the elementary algebra course.

A list compiled in the manner just described will be a list of all last year's graduates who were either in the top 15 per cent in scores on a test of scholastic aptitude, compared with a national sample of students, or among the high achievers in first-year algebra. Because many intelligence tests tend to give added weight to verbal abilities, addition of the high achievement in algebra criterion insures against overlooking some very able youngsters whose verbal skills are undeveloped. This list, then, will contain the names of most of the students in the class who could have been described as "high potential students" as they were entering high school four or five years ago. The major criterion used is that they should have earned scholastic aptitude test scores placing them in the highest 15 per cent of students tested in the *national norming sample*. This statement means that in one school there may be a very small percentage of academically talented students, whereas in another school half the class could be so labeled.

It is important to emphasize the comparison of students' test scores with the norms developed by the *publisher of the test*, rather than with school or local norms. Use of local norms or school distributions of scores in determining the identification of academically talented students can be very misleading and can cause serious misinterpretations of the study results, unless the distribution of academic talent in the school happens to be exactly the same as that in the test publisher's nationwide sample. *Use the publisher's norms.*

It is important also to note that in setting the criteria for identification of academically talented students only objectively determined criteria should be accepted. In the illustration, the criteria were scores above a certain level on scholastic aptitude tests *or* outstanding achievement in one mathematics course. No student should be included simply because some teachers think he is bright, or because he had a high grade average, or because he took advanced academic courses. The objective criteria such as test scores and Algebra I grades will not necessarily guarantee that *all* talented students will be included in the top 15 per cent, but clear, simple, and objective criteria are necessary to reduce the margin of error.

Obtaining the Data: The job to be done is one of finding the records of all students in last year's graduating class who met or surpassed the statistical definition of academically talented when they were in the eighth or ninth grade—then checking off the listed courses that each of these students took while in high school.

There are many possible ways to gather these data. The best way for a particular school is the *easiest* way; the choice of a method depends on how the student records are kept and who is to collect the data. One simple technique for obtaining and recording these data is described here to provide an illustration of a method that schools may revise and adapt to suit their own records and needs.

The Edge-Marked Card (An Illustration)

The edge-marked card technique provides an easy method for recording and analyzing a variety of data on a limited number of cases. It permits the recording of data by an untrained but careful and conscientious person, using forms the school can manufacture on its own duplicating machine. The technique yields complex analyses by *visual* means. Some care is needed in the design of the card so that every bit of information in which the school is interested will have a space for coding on the *edge* of the card, but a study of courses taken by a defined group of students should not tax the capacity of a card 5 inches by 8 inches. The figure on page 138 illustrates such a homemade card. Using the card shown below, the person tabulating the data goes through the following steps, making a separate numbered and marked card for every student in the class whose permanent record shows that he met either the test-score criterion or the algebra-grade criterion.

a. Write in the center part of the card

    1. The student's code number (probably his number in the class roster—or any number that will identify his name with his card if later checking is needed). The student's name is *not* listed on the card.

    2. The initials of the person marking the card.

    3. The name or initials of the scholastic aptitude test used as criterion, and the month and year administered.

b. With a colored pencil, mark each appropriate box with a firm stroke that goes off the *edge of the card*. (Marks that are straight, parallel with the limits of the box, and about midway between the edges of the box, make later counting of the marks easier.)

c. Mark first the box indicating *sex* of the student.

d. Mark next the box indicating test performance or algebra grade.

e. Mark next the appropriate box to show what is known about the student's post-high school career.

f. Turning the card so its long dimension is vertical, list the courses the student took in each of his four high school years and edge-mark the appropriate boxes. In order to reduce the amount of clerical work involved, a school might want to print the names of courses appropriate for each grade in the boxes and edge-mark those actually studied by the student.

g. The illustrative card shown here has a small box beside each course space in which the grade earned in a particular course may be noted. Grades are not necessary data in a study of this kind, but their notation on the cards may be useful for studies the school wishes to undertake later.

9th Grade—Listed Subjects Studied

10th Grade—Listed Subjects Studied

11th Grade—Listed Subjects Studied

12th Grade—Listed Subjects Studied

Post-High School Record

Enrolled in college
Other post-high school education
Military Service
Employed
Housewife (girl)
Unemployed
Unknown

School: _____
Class of: _____
Student's Code Number: _____
Coder's initials: _____

Sex	
Boy	
Girl	

Algebra I (95-100, A or A-)

TEST RANKING	
99-100%	
95- 98%	
90- 94%	
85- 89%	

Name of Test: _____

Test date: _____

138

Once cards have been marked for all students in the class who in the eighth or ninth grade met the criteria for classification as academically talented, it is a good practice to have a second person spot-check about 10 per cent of the cards for accuracy and completeness of marking. The results of the study can be no more accurate than the original coding made on these cards. When accuracy has been checked, the data on the cards are ready for analysis.

Analysis of edge-marked cards is a simple counting process. One can sort the cards and count marks very rapidly. The first step in an analysis of this kind probably will be a separation of the cards by sex, since final results will be more meaningful if the records of boys and girls are reported separately. Simply make sure that all cards face the same way and are right side up—then spread them along in a straight line so that just the edge (the edge with sex classification on it) of each card shows from beneath the card above it. The pencil marks for boys' cards will appear in one column; the marks for girls' cards in another. Separate the boys' cards from the girls' cards.

The next step is the analysis of the courses taken by the academically talented students. The procedure is simple: spread the cards again in a straight line so that just the edges with the pertinent information are revealed, and then count the marks for each course. Each school will design its own card to suit best its own needs and record-keeping system, but the method of the edge-marked card analysis remains the same.*

Interpreting the Results: When the counting has been completed, there will be a *number* for each listed course or sequence indicating the frequency with which that course has been taken by academically talented students in the group under study.

---

* The blank and unmarked card layout printed above may be used by any school, without special permission, in the manufacture of its own supply of cards:
    a. By tracing onto a mimeograph stencil, or
    b. By photographing the layout for offset reproduction.
Printed blank cards, exactly like that shown, may be purchased at nominal cost. Inquiries should be addressed to Study of the American High School, 20 Nassau Street, Princeton, New Jersey.

Interpretation and reporting of such numbers can be undertaken in any manner the school prefers. Often results such as these are most easily interpreted if they are converted to proportions (percentages) and expressed graphically as shown on p. 28.

About the author

Dr. James Bryant Conant was born in Massachusetts in 1893. He was educated at Harvard University, where in 1919 he became an assistant professor of chemistry. By 1931, he was head of the chemistry department, and in 1933 he was chosen president of the University, a position he held until he retired in 1953.

During World War I, Dr. Conant worked in the Chemical Warfare Service. He served in World War II as advisor to the Manhattan project, which produced the first atomic bomb; from 1947 through 1952 he was a member of the General Advisory Committee of the Atomic Energy Commission. He was sent to Germany in February, 1953, as U.S. High Commissioner, a post he retained until after the formal occupation was terminated, when President Eisenhower appointed him U.S. Ambassador to the Federal Republic of Germany. He resigned in early 1957.

His current two-year study of the American public high school, under a grant from the Carnegie Corporation administered by the Educational Testing Service of Princeton, New Jersey, culminates a long interest in public education which has manifested itself throughout the years in a number of provocative articles and books on the topic.

Dr. Conant is the author of a number of books, including *Germany and Freedom, Education in a Divided World, Education and Liberty, On Understanding Science,* and *Modern Science and Modern Man.*